WRITING
THE NORTHWEST

WRITING
THE NORTHWEST

A Reporter Looks Back

HILL WILLIAMS

foreword by Jim Kershner

WSU
PRESS

Washington State University Press
Pullman, Washington

WSU PRESS
WASHINGTON STATE UNIVERSITY

Washington State University Press
PO Box 645910
Pullman, Washington 99164-5910
Phone: 800-354-7360
Fax: 509-335-8568
Email: wsupress@wsu.edu
Website: wsupress.wsu.edu

Library of Congress Cataloging-in-Publication Data

Names: Williams, Hill, 1926- author.
Title: Writing the Northwest : a reporter looks back / by Hill Williams ;
    foreword by Jim Kershner.
Description: Pullman, Washington : Washington State University Press, 2017. |
    Includes bibliographical references and index.
Identifiers: LCCN 2016047757 | ISBN 9780874223453 (alk. paper)
Subjects: LCSH: Williams, Hill, 1926- | Journalists--United States--Biography.
Classification: LCC PN4874.W624 A3 2017 | DDC 070.92 [B] --dc23
LC record available at https://lccn.loc.gov/2016047757

Contents

Foreword, by Jim Kershner   vii

Introduction: All the Birds in the Sky   ix

The Williams Family Arrives in Washington   1

Growing Up in Pasco   9

Early Journalism   19

Seattle and the *Times*   35

People   49

Cold War Years   61

Geology   79

At Sea in the Pacific Northwest   99

On Land in the Pacific Northwest   111

A Northwesterner in the Far East   141

Japan and World War II   167

Index   171

Foreword

by Jim Kershner

SETTLE IN FOR AN ENTERTAINING and wide-ranging trip into the Northwest's history and prehistory, with Hill Williams as your avuncular tour guide. A more knowledgeable companion would be hard to find. Williams has especially strong credentials for leading this journey. First, he was born and raised in the center of Washington, which means he understands both the wet *and* dry sides of the state, a perspective less common than you might imagine. Second, he spent decades roaming the region as the *Seattle Times*' science reporter, seeking out experts on geology, anthropology, and just about every scientific subject in between. As a result, Williams combines a native-born son's intuitive understanding with a scientist's restless curiosity and deep knowledge.

The word "vignette" might be more apt than the word "story" to describe many of these pieces. Most have the virtue of brevity. Some do not even have a story's traditional beginning, middle, and ending. I had to dig into my roots as a theater reviewer to come up with the best description for a few of these pieces: They reminded me of "memory plays," conjuring a time, a place, and a life. His tales of growing up in the Tri-Cities gave me a feel for what life was like on the dry banks of the Columbia—as well as a feel for the forces that shaped Hill Williams. His anecdotes of working as a cub reporter there depict a colorful—now vanished—time in that profession. Yet these vignettes go deeper. His story about a turkey giveaway captures the tenor and mood of Washington in the Great Depression better than any facts and figures.

In other hands, these tales might have been gauzy or sentimental, yet Williams brings a considerable practical advantage. He simply knows more about Northwest and natural history than most laymen. His knowledge has impressive breadth, gleaned from decades of observing hundreds of scientists and researchers doing fascinating work. Throughout his career, he has proven to be an expert interviewer and expert interpreter of sometimes impenetrable scientific and academic jargon. His years of daily journalism training honed his skills at sharing arcane knowledge simply and concisely. Several stories are explicitly about Northwest natural history, focusing on places like Celilo Falls and Kamiak Butte, for example. Many are based on reporting trips, including a whaling expedition with the Makah tribe, and a hike on the hot rocks of Mount St. Helens—accounts that convey a basic understanding of the science and history of the subject, yet also accomplish something even more valuable. They put us there, along with Hill Williams, in the middle of Northwest history.

I know of few books that touch upon such a wide variety of regional topics, from basalt outcrops to atomic bombs to salmon runs to scablands. I finished this book having learned plenty about my home state. Mainly, however, I finished it with plenty of affection for our tour guide. I've never met Hill Williams, but after reading this collection, I feel that I have.

Jim Kershner is a senior correspondent with the Spokane *Spokesman Review*. He is a staff historian with HistoryLink.org, the Online Encyclopedia of Washington State History. He has won seven awards from the National Society of Newspaper Columnists. His most recent book is *Carl Maxey: A Fighting Life* (University of Washington Press, 2008).

Introduction

~

All the Birds in the Sky

As I look back on my career in journalism, I realize many of my stories were reflections of how the world was changing—bits of history, although I may not have realized it.

My stories, written over the course of four decades, now offer historical glimpses in addition to newsworthy accounts of their time and place. Most were about our Pacific Northwest and scientific revelations, others quick glimpses of life in other countries—reflections of how the world was changing, events that many of us have forgotten or are too young to remember. Perhaps some of these bits of history will fill in gaps of our understanding of why the world is the way it is.

Throughout the years my readers and editors took the time to remind me that a journalist's work, though important and of real value to the public, deserves a critical review.

I remember a commercial airliner many years ago falling short of its destination at Sea-Tac Airport and splashing into Puget Sound near Tacoma. Passengers and crew were rescued, although some got wet. I was interviewing passengers for the *Seattle Times* in a Tacoma hospital later that day and a little Chinese girl was chattering at me. I glanced at an interpreter who translated: "All the birds in the sky fell in the sea and were drowned."

I liked the rhythm and used it in my story. The city editor liked it, too. He told me: "You seem to do better when you can't understand what they're saying."

The Williams Family Arrives in Washington

I DROVE TO WILSON CREEK, a tiny town in central Washington, in the mid-1990s to see where the Great Northern Railway delivered the Williams family to the Pacific Northwest a century earlier. It was warm and sunny, perhaps like the day in April 1902, when my father, Hill, eight years old, scrambled off what the locals called an immigrant train.

My dad would have been happy that the long, cross-country trip was over—and probably full of curiosity about the new country. But I wondered about his parents' reaction to the country. My grandparents, William L. Williams, 40, a tall, strong, serious man, and Christie Simpson Williams, 34, a warmer, affectionate person, had left a farm overlooking the Strawberry River in northwest Arkansas where distant hills were forested. Not a really prosperous farm, but a dependable living.

As they stepped off the train in Wilson Creek, the first thing they would have seen was a long, black wall of lava rock right along the tracks. And beyond, bare, dry hills with more outcrops of that black rock.

My grandfather wouldn't have shown emotion. He would have been efficient and maybe a little gruff as he rounded up his family's possessions, even farm tools that had been carried in boxcars the "immigrants" had rented. He may have brought livestock in boxcars the immigrant could rent for animals. If so, one of my Dad's chores would have been tending them on the long trip west.

Christie, my grandmother, would have gathered possessions for the dozen-mile wagon ride to Ephrata where my
grandfather had arranged temporary accommodations. I
wondered if she was thinking of family and friends they'd left
behind, and of the farm and the nearby town with churches,
stores, and friends' homes.

For my grandparents the hardest to leave behind must
have been the graves of their three children—Wendell, Milton and Alma—all of them dead before the age of two.

I also wondered if the train crew might have been at least
a little relieved to unload passengers in Wilson Creek. There
were four Williams-related families aboard, including 20
cousins, seemingly a recipe for chaos.

The road to Ephrata wound through some of the most des-
olate country in the state—more jagged, black rock, sandy
hills, sparse sagebrush. My grandmother must have been
wondering what god-forsaken country they were going to
live in. If my grandfather felt discouraged, he wouldn't have
shown it.

Eight-year-old Hill was probably watching for cowboys or
Indians. He had been in charge of the family's long rifle on
the trip west and remembered carrying it, wrapped in paper,
through a crowded Great Northern depot in Spokane as they
changed trains. He was a good shot when I knew him and
apparently had been as a boy.

Wilson Creek was in a channel carved by a great ice-age
flood thousands of years before, though no one yet realized
it. The newcomers probably would have scoffed if anyone
had mentioned a flood in that dry country.

The family spent the summer and winter in Ephrata while
Will scouted the country on horseback looking for land, still
largely unmarked. Township corners were marked, but the

markers were six miles apart and the homesteader had to locate his claim by measuring off from those markers. There were people in the country with rudimentary surveying skills who would help a homesteader locate a claim and my grandfather may have hired one of them.

Homesteaders had been settling eastern Washington for 15 or 20 years before the Williamses arrived in 1902 and the best land had been claimed—the Palouse country, the Walla Walla Valley, and stream bottoms. Available land was farther west in the Big Bend of the Columbia River.

Under the Homestead Act, any citizen or one who declared an intention to become one, who was head of a family or a single man over 21, could obtain 160 acres of government land free except for a $10 filing fee. The homesteader was required to establish a home on the land within six months and have 10 acres under cultivation by the second year and another 20 acres each following year. After five years, the land was his.

Transfer of title from the United States to William L. Williams is recorded in the Douglas County courthouse in Waterville, dated 1907. (The land, in what is known as the Quincy Flats, is now in Grant County, formed from the eastern part of Douglas County in 1909.)

The settler's first job was to grub out the sagebrush, a tough job as anyone who's done it will remember. I wouldn't be surprised if my grandfather hooked up a horse to pull out the biggest ones. It was a woman's job to put in a garden, so Christie would have done that, possibly grubbing out sagebrush herself. It would have been the first time Christie heard the clear, musical call of the western meadowlark, one of the delights of the dry country. Eastern meadowlarks in Arkansas lacked the melodic double-noted call of the western birds.

In that treeless country, they used sagebrush for fuel. It burns hot and fast, requiring constant resupplying and producing smoke of a distinctive, pungent smell you never forget. Until my grandfather drilled a well, they either hauled water from the river or paid a dollar a barrel for water from an eight-barrel wagon pulled by a four-horse team.

My grandfather sold the farm in 1910 and the family moved to Pullman so Hill, then in high school, could attend college. My grandfather got a job in Washington State College's agricultural nursery. The school was just 20 years old.

My parents, Hill Williams and Ursula Trainor, met in 1920 when they were teaching in schools in the Palouse Country. They were married in 1922 and moved to Pasco where my father had been hired as principal of Pasco High School.

He had been editor of the college paper at Washington State, the *Evergreen*. So maybe it's not surprising that he resigned the school job and bought a half interest in the weekly *Pasco Herald* a year or so later. He later acquired the other half interest and was editor and publisher until shortly before his death in 1948.

You don't survive long as a weekly newspaper owner unless you devote much of your time to the business side. I was at the other end. They paid me to do what I loved.

I like to think of my father's entry to the newspaper business as the spark that started us on our long journeys in news, channeling our lives through an amazing period in history.

I lucked into my first job on a weekly paper in 1948 and my luck held for more than 40 years. Through all those years and newspapers, I had the most interesting jobs.

❧   ❧   ❧

The Trainor farm near Rosalia Washington. *Author photo.*

My parents' youthful years were in the Palouse Country, their homes nestled in the serene, green hills that stretch off to the horizon.

My mother, Ursula Trainor, remembered rising at dawn on her family's farm to bake pies for the big mid-day meal for the harvest workers. She preferred working during the cool, early mornings and having the afternoons for reading. Her sisters preferred to sleep later.

My father, Hill Williams Sr., "punched header" during harvests during his college years in Pullman, a skilled job that not only involved managing a team of horses, but adjusting the cutting head for the height of grain and the slope they were working on. Oh, yes—and preventing the whole rig from tipping over on the steepest hills. Even today visitors

Harvest on the Palouse. *Courtesy, Sam Pambrun collection.*

sometimes wonder what keeps harvesting equipment, now pulled by tractors rather than horses, from rolling down those steep slopes.

❧   ❧   ❧

In the early days of aviation—with lower, slower planes— pilots found their way by watching the ground, often following rivers, railroads or highways. If clouds or fog hid the ground, they didn't fly. Neither did they fly on dark, moonless nights and that was a handicap to the first attempts in 1918 to establish air mail. In those days, it took railroads 108 hours to carry a letter across the United States. A combination of trains and planes—mail going by air during the day, transferred to a train at sunset and back to a plane at dawn— cut the time to 78 hours. But still not fast enough to interest

Congress in funding air mail. So the Postal Service tried an experiment.

At 6 A.M. on February 22, 1921, two planes took off from a field in San Francisco and headed east. Relay pilots and planes were ready at scheduled refueling stops. When night fell, the flight continued, guided by bonfires or temporary flares. (The flight was soon down to one plane; the other had crashed at Elko, Nevada, killing the pilot.) The most spectacular leg of the flight was from North Platte, Nebraska, to Chicago with stops in Omaha and Iowa City. It was cold and began to snow. The pilot, James H. Knight, was guided across the dark, frozen prairie by bonfires, flaming oil drums, and flares, tended by farmers, postal employees, and other volunteers. He landed in Chicago and another pilot finished the flight to New York City. But the press made a hero of Knight because of the difficulty of his flight—and the fact that, aside from the bonfires, he had navigated with only a small compass and a torn-out section of a road map. Think of that the next time you are flying five miles high in a plane that is tracked by radar with your pilot constantly in touch with controllers on the ground.

Seven pilots had taken part in the 2,629-mile flight. It took 33 hours and 20 minutes from San Francisco to New York City. (Of that, only 26 hours had been spent in the air.) It prompted Congress to begin funding air mail. And in the mid-1920s the government began building a nationwide network of aviation-navigation beacons, spaced 15 to 25 miles apart, bright enough to be seen 40 miles in clear weather.

There was one of those beacons on Jump-Off Joe, the highest hill above Kennewick across the Columbia River from our home in Pasco, Washington. And in the winter, when leaves were off the trees, we could see its flashes from home. The lights didn't actually flash like today's strobe lights; the beam rotated, aimed a few degrees above horizontal, so you'd see it as the beam swept past you. The beacons also had red and green lights that would flash 180 degrees behind the white light, although we couldn't see those from home. They were coded to give pilots an idea of where they were on the lighted flight path.

Sometimes when my siblings and I were little and were waiting for Dad to come home from work, our mother would tell us stories or read to us. And if it was dark and the leaves were gone, we'd see that flashing beacon on Jump-Off Joe.

One of the stories our mother told concerned the year she took off from teaching to be home on the family farm while her father, Will Trainor, was dying of a then-mysterious disease, probably multiple sclerosis, that caused progressive paralysis but left his mind clear. One sunny day as he lay in bed, she had filled his pipe and was reading to him.

They could hear an airplane, one of few in that country at the time, but couldn't see it from the window. Suddenly, the plane's shadow flashed across the bed. The usually garrulous old Irishman was silent for a moment as he drew on his pipe and then said, "Think of that. I didn't see the machine but its shadow flew across my bed."

Will Trainor died May 19, 1920, age 61.

Growing up in Pasco

M Y FRIENDS AND I couldn't appreciate how tough times were in the Great Depression.

Pasco, my home town in southeast Washington, had a population of about 3,000 in the 1930s. Around 1937, when I would have been 11 years old, the Pasco Chamber of Commerce had a tradition of giving away live turkeys to a downtown crowd a few days before Thanksgiving. The birds were released from atop a wooden tower, maybe 50 feet high, near the old City Hall. The birds would flutter 30 yards or so across a block that was then mostly vacant. Whoever caught a bird took it home.

As I remember, there were about 50 men and a scattering of kids who would rush after each bird. The day had been fairly uneventful, although we saw a man take a turkey away from the kid who had caught it. It made us mad. What we didn't realize was that many of these men were desperate, out of work, with no money and a family to feed.

The people in charge made the mistake of announcing that they were about to release the last turkey. There was a mad rush as the doomed bird fluttered to the ground. I never did see the guy who caught it because he was immediately surrounded by a knot of pursuers trying to get at the turkey, a packed mass of struggling men, maybe 20 or 25 of them.

I made a run at the rim, trying to wedge between bodies. A big guy grabbed my collar and shoved me back saying: "That's no place for a boy." He was right.

The struggle over the turkey continued for several minutes. Finally, a group of police and volunteer firemen formed a line with the point man knocking heads as he forced a way toward the center. (The point man was Robert "Pepper" Martin—volunteer fireman, fresh from University of Washington football, a reporter at the *Pasco Herald*—my hero.) There wasn't enough left of the turkey to worry about by the time the group was split apart.

I don't remember anyone being arrested. Police gave people more leeway then than they do now and the cops probably understood why it happened. The Chamber of Commerce learned its lesson. That was Pasco's last Thanksgiving turkey release.

My mother wept when I told her about it. I thought she was sad that I didn't get a turkey. I know now that she was weeping for those desperate men and their families. I'm sure we had a good meal that night, not fancy but adequate. It may have been what my mother called slumgullion, a tasty and probably nutritious combination of whatever we happened to have in the house.

[I wrote this story for the *Seattle Times* in 1968. It ran on page 1 on Thanksgiving Day. Not all the readers liked it. A Seattle woman wrote that it was "indicative of the low literary values of the man who wrote it and the shockingly poor taste of the editors who gave it a place of prominence."]

❧   ❧   ❧

My friends and I would occasionally hike from Pasco out to a swimming hole on the Snake River we called Locust Grove. A few spindly locust trees, maybe, but certainly no grove. The hike, several miles each way, was mostly over sagebrush-spotted sand, past abandoned farms that were sad reminders of failed efforts to grow crops without irrigation.

A railroad track ran along a bluff above Locust Grove—the old Spokane, Portland & Seattle Railway. We were hiking home from Locust Grove one day when a freight train passed by, very slowly. Men were looking out of empty boxcars and a few were sitting on flatcars. That was the way many jobless men traveled, looking for work—until a railway cop would throw them off at the next town.

Inexplicably, we began throwing rocks at the men. I still don't know why. They were probably broke, away from home and lonely, maybe sick, unemployed, probably wondering where the next meal would come from. We were young and healthy, had homes to go to, an assured meal that night. But we were kids, and we threw rocks.

Then, to our horror, the train stopped and some of the younger men jumped off and began chasing us. I'm sure the stop was for a railroad reason, not to get us, but it didn't make much difference that day. We were scared. We easily outdistanced them in the soft sand. Maybe they didn't really want to catch us.

I made a hard day even harder for those unfortunate men.

❧   ❧   ❧

It's surprising, even to me, to remember that I had a *Saturday Evening Post* route in my early teens. The *Post* was a popular weekly magazine before television, before computers, before iPhones. It featured news, short stories, humor, commentary by famous authors, and articles aimed at women, mostly at home in those days. Many saved and framed the magazine covers, often by Norman Rockwell.

I don't think I had very many regular customers, but I'd walk through the lobby of the old Pasco Hotel and usually sell all I had left over. Once, on roller skates, the bag of magazines and I bumped into the back of a dignified visitor at the hotel. I don't remember if he purchased a magazine. Probably not.

Bob Skill, in his late teens, was the *Post* dealer in Pasco. The magazine price in those years was 5 cents a copy! I don't remember what I paid Bob so I don't know how many pennies I made from each sale. But I won a sales prize: a hunting knife with leather sheath. I still have it.

By 1946, long after I had gone on to other things, the *Post's* price was up to 10 cents an issue. The magazine died in 1969.

❦   ❦   ❦

I had a kayak in my high-school years, a little one maybe eight feet long, wood frame covered with canvas, purchased from Zane Casey, a classmate who'd built it. (I wasn't particularly good at building things.)

Sometimes in the summer I'd load it on the car and after breakfast Dad would drive me up the river to a place across from Richland where I'd launch the boat. Dad would drive back to town and go to work. And I would set off on a day-long drift.

The river was empty then. I'd rarely see another boat. And the river was still free flowing: McNary Dam was more than a decade in the future. The current was swift enough to create eddies and whirlpools that would twirl the kayak. It was fun. It was so quiet I could hear the water rustling against the canvas.

I would drift past mostly empty river banks. Today's nice homes along the river hadn't been built. I would drift past Kennewick and Pasco, under the old highway bridge and the Northern Pacific Railway bridge. And then late in the afternoon I'd paddle to shore at Sacajawea State Park where the muddy Snake River joins the blue Columbia. And my patient dad, on his way home from work, would pick me up and I'd be home in time for dinner.

From a kid's standpoint, life then was quiet, slow, and carefree. I'm not sure my parents and their friends would have agreed with the carefree part. They were still struggling with the aftereffects of the Great Depression, and more aware than I of the raging world war that was not going well for the United States, a conflict that would soon sweep all of us into a world changed forever.

☙   ☙   ☙

Olav Skartland, my friend since third grade, and I were both home in Pasco on leave from the Navy in 1944. Olav was in flight training and far enough along that he could rent a plane.

So one afternoon he and I went to an airfield on the hill behind Kennewick and rented a two-seat, open-cockpit plane. He was in front at the controls.

After we gained altitude, Olav began flight maneuvers. I was relaxing, enjoying the view when I suddenly looked over my head, straight down at sagebrush far below. We were in a slow loop that had me upside down hanging by the seat belt. Startled, I grabbed the seat with both hands, although by that time it would have been a bit late if my belt had come loose or I had forgotten to fasten it.

Right side up again, Olav tapped the side of his head which I learned later was a signal to the "student" to take control. I continued to enjoy the view as the plane began to point lower and off to the side. Finally, Olav jerked it back to steady flight. He said later, "I wondered what you were trying to do." The answer: Nothing.

We decided to fly over our homes in Pasco and see if we could get our families to look up. We zoomed low over the Skartland house at 5 A Street, but no one came out, or maybe no one was there. Then we flew the few blocks to 202 North 8th Street to see if we could rouse my family.

As it happened, my dad was in our backyard talking to one of his printers. We zoomed low and I leaned out and waved. The printer said to my dad, "I wonder who that damn fool is." My dad, who had recognized my jacket, said "I'm afraid I know."

The Kennewick police were waiting for us when we returned to the airfield. They said there were complaints we were flying too low, endangering people and violating the law. When they learned that Olav was a Navy flyer, they cautioned him not to do it again, at least over Kennewick, and did not write a ticket.

❦   ❦   ❦

Computers have probably banished time clocks to the past along with slide rules and pencil sharpeners. I punched one briefly during my last year in college.

My friend, Al Duclos, and I shared a room at the University of Washington's Newman Club. We were both on the GI Bill and looking for ways to reduce expenses. We cut our rent in half by keeping the building clean, but wanted better meals than we were able to prepare.

We found jobs at the university's Commons (now Raitt Hall) that had, in addition to a cafeteria-style dining area for students, a fancier dining room for groups such as the Board of Regents. The job waiting on tables in the dining area not only paid a little but included a free meal.

Al and I would pull our time cards from a rack on the time clock, push them in a slot, hear a click as the machine stamped our arrival time, replace the cards in the rack and sit down to a really good meal before beginning work. That went on a few times until the dietician told us firmly to punch in AFTER the meal, not before. They were still good meals.

Dave Beck, head of the Teamsters Union, was a member of the Board of Regents that year. I remember he was the only one who said "thank you" when I set a plate in front of him.

❧   ❧   ❧

In the summer of 1947 my friend Mike Hughes and I went to LaPush, on the Olympic Peninsula at the western edge of Washington State, to look for jobs on salmon-fishing boats. For almost a week in the summer of 1947 the wind had kept the salmon-fishing boats idle in the mouth of the Quillayute River. It is a short river, composed of turbulent streams tumbling down the west side of the Olympic Mountains that unite to flow a few dignified miles to the Pacific Ocean. James Island, small, steep, and topped by a fringe of battered trees, sits squarely in the mouth of the river, taming the heaving swells as they surge in from the Pacific.

It's a good place for small boats to hole up in a blow. But fishing boats are not made to be tied up in a river, and fishermen are not psychologically equipped to be ashore day after day.

But this evening the clouds had parted, just long enough for the sun's last yellow light to throw shadows in the little town of LaPush. Fishermen stood on the dock, hands deep in pockets, squinting at the sky and sniffing the wind. Things looked and smelled better. Small-craft warnings were still flying at the Coast Guard station, but the radio had said the warnings would come down in a few hours.

The sea takes a few days to get over a storm. And although it looked as though fishing would be possible the next day, the men would take a beating in the small boats. These were trollers that dragged multiple lines from poles angling out on each side. The men work in a cockpit at the stern, handling lines, managing the mechanical reels that pull in lines, gaffing the hooked fish and tossing them in a box for cleaning. The cockpit is about hip deep and when a man stands to boat a fish his hands are too full of line, gaff, and fish to hang on to anything else. So when a swell surges up under the stern, lifts it high and then suddenly drops out from under it, legs and hips take a beating as the fisherman bounces around in the cockpit.

Bruises are OK if you're making money. But Ole Westby of the boat *Penguin* commented: "Vell, Ay tink the vedder be good enough tomorrow to keep lines in the water. But Ay damn if Ay get black and blue for no fish."

No one had done well this year, even hard workers like Mike Walsh on the *Rose* and Moe Thompson on the *Spray*. Only one boat had bothered to go out on this day. It wasn't even a troller, just a gillnetter from the Columbia River. The two crewmen stowed the gillnets and used hand lines over the stern.

The little boat came into sight just as the last sliver of sun slipped into the sea. It was rolling mightily and regularly dropped from sight in the trough of big rollers. It finally reached smoother water inside of James Island and began plowing up the river to the scow where fish were unloaded. The tide was running out so the gillnetter made slow progress as it plowed past the forest of poles on the idle trollers.

When trollers are fishing, the poles—two at midships and two smaller ones forward—lie out at an angle over the water, and the boats look stable and graceful. In port when the poles are up, the gracefulness is gone. They look top-heavy and cluttered.

Ordinarily, everyone would crowd the dock to see what the incoming boat had, but only a few bothered this time. On a day when the 40-footers stayed in, anyone on a tiny, tossing gillnetter should just hang on and forget about fishing.

A blonde giant on the dock bellowed across the water to the boat, "How much you got?"

"Fifty-one," one of them shouted back.

"Pounds?"

"No. Fish!"

Fifty-one fish! Why, they'd been out only half a day. The salmon must be here. Word spread to the store in a series of yells and soon even the proprietor was scrambling down the ladder to the fish deck. Sure enough, a heap of fish glistened on the gillnetter's deck, both big spotted Chinook and the smaller, brighter silvers.

The tired fishermen, big grins on their wind-burned faces, were throwing fish onto the scow where the fish-grader sorted them and threw them on the scales, calling out weights through a wad of chewing tobacco.

Men took one look and started for their boats to check gear, fuel, supplies, take on ice, and get to bed early. Boats cut loose from nests at the dock and anchored in mid-stream so they could take off early without waiting for those tied up outside them. The next morning, long before the sun got up to look at the little settlement it had left so slow moving the night before, the roar of engines filled the air. By 3 A.M. the river was deserted by all but the scow and the store.

Salmon had come back to the Quillayute—and I had a job as a boat puller on the boat *Goldenrod,* landing fish with mechanical reels, cleaning them, throwing guts and gills overboard where seagulls quickly snapped them up, icing down the fish, cleaning the boat of fish slime, cooking meals, and sometimes taking the helm.

In the following summer of 1948 I could have found another fishing job, but had graduated from the University of Washington and had a job—a newspaper job.

Early Journalism

THE NEWSPAPER JOBS I HAD in the early 1940s are gone. The half-century I worked on newspapers—both large and small—saw a fundamental change in how newspapers are put together and printed.

In those days, small weekly newspapers were printed directly from hundreds of pieces of lead that printers laboriously assembled—individual lines of type for news stories and blocks of lead for advertisements and illustrations. They were locked in a frame the size of a newspaper page. It was flat; ink was applied and paper printed directly from it.

These days, news stories are written, edited, and provided headlines on computer screens. Advertisements are made up and pages are put together on screen and sent electronically to the presses. Clattering typewriters are gone from newsrooms. Newspapers have become quiet places.

And we're witnessing another big change—the familiar printed-on-paper newspapers now supplemented and even substituted by on-screen versions that eliminate the need for delivery drivers and delivery persons. But I'm a lot better at remembering how things were than predicting the future of newspapers.

My first employer was the *Pasco Herald,* a weekly newspaper owned by my father, Hill Williams Sr. It was wartime and printers were in short supply, so I worked there part time during my last years of high school in the early 1940s.

One of my jobs was melting a big pot of lead over a gas flame, recycling the soft metal that had been used in the last

Four type slugs set on the Linotype. *Courtesy Deepwood Press, Mancelona, Michigan.*

A Linotype machine. *Courtesy Wikimedia Commons.*

week's paper or in printing jobs. It was inky and a little oily so I'd need to skim off the scum that formed as it melted. I still remember the smell from the gas flame, the scum, and the lead itself at more than 620 degrees Fahrenheit.

The Linotype machines that cast molten lead into lines of type for news stories were fed by big slugs of lead. I made those. We called them pigs and they were 18 to 20 inches long—and heavy. They had a loop at one end so the Linotype operator could hang them on a hook that lowered them, inch by inch, into the machine where they would melt and be cast into lines of type.

Using a big ladle, I'd pour molten metal into forms to make the pigs. I worked very, very carefully, remembering that a predecessor on that job had slopped molten lead into his shoe.

I also poured the molds that were used for illustrations in advertisements. I would lock a heavy cardboard-like mat in a vertical position in a mold. Then I poured molten lead through a narrow slot in the top. It had to be a continuous pour to avoid a disfiguring line in the casting. Then, after a few minutes, I used heavy gloves to remove the casting and put in another mat and do it again.

I sawed the castings to remove excess metal—which went back in the pot—so the cut, as we called it, would fit in the advertisement the printers were putting together.

The cuts, along with hundreds of lines of type and other pieces of lead and wooden spacing, would be locked into a metal frame called the chase. The chase was on a table with a stone top that provided a flat surface to make up a page. Everything, lines of type, my cuts, had to fit exactly and that was worrisome because I had trouble sawing anything square. Still do.

Once made up, the page was locked tightly in place with wedges called quoins (pronounced "coins"). Then it had to be carried to the press. It was heavy. Type-high is 0.918 inch, so two of us would carry a newspaper-size slab of lead almost an inch thick. The chase was just a frame—it didn't have a bottom. The only thing holding all that type and cuts in place was pressure from the quoins.

If a cut wasn't square—and some of mine weren't—there was a danger something would come loose as we carried it to the press and the whole page would fall to the floor—a pile of hundreds of pieces of lead, what the printers called pied type. Lead is a soft metal, and dropping it often damaged the type or cuts. You can imagine the mess and the task of putting it back together—and the dark looks I got.

We put four pages, each locked in a chase, on the press, known for obvious reasons as a flat-bed press. A big, drum-like roller came around and grabbed a single sheet of paper the size of four pages from a platform on top of the press and carried it around to print directly from the type. And that meant that someone, usually me, was feeding those sheets.

To get ready, I lugged as big a stack of those sheets—the size of four newspaper pages—as I could manage up a few steps and flopped it down atop the press.

The trick was to flip the top sheet to get air under it so it would slide easily to where clips on the roller could grab it. As the roller took the single sheet around to print from the forms, I'd flip the next sheet to position it for the next time the roller came around. The press printed a sheet about every two seconds.

If I got distracted and didn't position the sheet perfectly, the clips would catch only a corner and the whole sheet would tear and distribute itself in postage-stamp size pieces

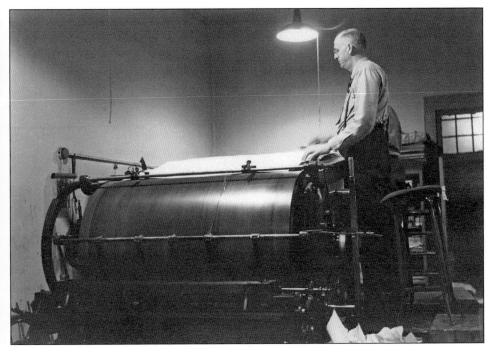

Hill Williams Sr. feeds the press at the *Pasco Herald* in this 1942 photo. *Author photo.*

on the ink rollers. It made a loud ripping noise and I'd see Dad, working in the front office, wince at the thought of the delay as I tromped on the brake and climbed down to pick inky black shreds of newsprint off the rollers.

After the first run, we'd turn the sheets over and run them through again with new pages the printers had prepared. Most of the year the paper had eight pages so two press runs did it. On the second run, we'd hook up a mechanical folder that would cut and fold the sheets.

Press night was Thursday. After the press runs, we'd address the papers (Joe Blow, Pasco, was all the address needed then) and get them to the post office for local distribution and in time to catch the train up the county to Connell and Kahlotus. If we were late (if I'd torn too many sheets on the press), we'd drive the papers up the county.

People depended on the *Pasco Herald.* In the Great Depression when they couldn't afford the $2 yearly subscription they might pay with a bag of wheat or potatoes. Dad always accepted such payments. Our family could use the potatoes. I'm not sure what he did with the wheat. I remember sacks of wheat stacked in the back room near my melting pot. Rats got in there so someone set traps. A highlight, for me at least, was when a printer stepped in a trap.

I was paid 10 cents an hour. It made it easy to figure my time sheet. Years later, on my first job as a reporter, the *Kennewick Courier-Reporter* paid me a solid dollar an hour.

❧   ❧   ❧

I walked into the *Kennewick Courier-Reporter* office in the spring of 1948 looking for my first newspaper reporting job. I was hopeful but, realistically, not too hopeful. I had already looked for newspaper jobs on both sides of the Cascades without success.

I didn't have a car and it seemed as though a newspaper reporter should have a car. Despite a brand-new diploma in journalism from the University of Washington, I didn't have clippings to prove I'd ever written anything for a newspaper.

But I was lucky. The editor and publisher, Rolf W. Tuve, thought he had hired a reporter the week before, but the young man never showed up. I got the job, a peculiar way to begin more than 40 years of writing news during an amazing time in history, almost half a century of work that was interesting, sometimes exciting, never boring.

Tuve had bought the *Courier-Reporter* in 1945 from Ralph E. Reed, owner since 1910. But like many in the newspaper business, Reed couldn't stay away from the old place and was there often keeping an eye on things, including the new reporter.

The job was a good start for me. Kennewick in 1948 was small enough that I walked almost everywhere I needed to go, rarely needing to borrow a car. Reed and my father, Hill Williams Sr., who had been editor and publisher of the weekly *Pasco Herald* across the Columbia River from Kennewick, were long-time, friendly competitors. And Reed's son Jim, who like me had grown up in his dad's newspaper shop, was home from the Army working as a printer for Tuve.

I happily went to work.

❦   ❦   ❦

In those days, small shops like the *Courier-Reporter* occasionally attracted a wandering printer looking for work. One of them walked in one day when the paper needed an extra hand and Tuve hired him on the spot, the same way he hired me.

They were known as tramp printers. They could set type by hand; they knew how to operate a Linotype. They could set up a printing job and run the press. They were journeymen in their craft. The term "tramp printer" was not derogatory; they were skilled, valued craftsmen. But they couldn't settle down.

Memories of tramp printers remind me of lines from Robert Service:

> *There's a race of men that don't fit in,*
> *A race that can't stay still....*

The owner of a print shop or small newspaper often would welcome a printer who showed up unannounced looking for work. If he (and occasionally she) was needed, he'd put on an apron and go to work in a shop that would be almost identical in layout and equipment to print shops anywhere. But tramp printers belong to the past. Computers and ever improving software changed printing technology in the 1960s and '70s, eliminating their jobs, ending their usefulness.

The printer didn't carry tools or equipment. He carried knowledge and skills in a day when his industry hadn't changed much in a century. But soon enough the itchy feet that brought him to the shop would bother him again. Often the boss would hate to see him go but go he would, satisfying the recurring restlessness, eventually showing up at another shop perhaps across the country.

He's a rolling stone, and it's bred in the bone;
He's a man who won't fit in.

It's tempting to compare tramp printers of the past to today's computer wonks, information technologists who don't have to lug computers from job to job, only their skills. But our society discourages wandering journeymen. Health plans, pensions, and 401(k)s tend to hold workers in place.

Some tramp printers were alcoholics, working until a drinking binge would end the job. That happened at the *Courier-Reporter* while I was there. The next day Jim suggested that he and I each give the hung-over man $5 to help him get out of town. I guess I hesitated (at $40 a week, $5 seemed like a lot of money), because Jim responded: "Our dads would do it." So we did.

In 1949, only a year after I was hired, the *Kennewick Courier-Reporter* went out of existence when its assets were acquired by the *Tri-City Herald*.

❧   ❧   ❧

I shot my own news photographs as a reporter on the *Tri-City Herald* in the late 1940s and early 1950s. I used the big Speed Graphic camera that was in widespread use at that time. Compared to the slick little digital cameras of today, the old Speed Graphic seems like a dinosaur. It weighed more than four pounds and required both hands to use it.

But it was the news camera from the 1920s through the 1950s, the most-used still camera of World War II. Over time it was replaced first by small 35-millimeter cameras, and then by digital.

O.K., let's say you want to make a news photograph the way we used to.

The Speed Graphic had a carrying strap and if you needed to climb something you could slip your belt through the strap. I did that once going up a ladder on an oil-storage tank, the camera bumping my behind as I climbed.

The Speed Graphic used individual sheets of film, usually 4 x 5 inches, that would be loaded in film holders in a darkroom before you started out. Two sheets of film in a holder, one on each side. A thin, metal film stop slid in each side to keep light from the film. The whole thing, the loaded film holder, slid into a spring-loaded attachment on the back of the camera, seating itself with a satisfying clunk.

Now to take the photograph: Pull out the film stop so the image can reach the film. If you forget to do this...well, more times than I like to remember I got back with blank film.

There is an optical viewfinder atop the camera and, for fast action, a wire frame that flips up to roughly frame your scene.

Now to take the picture—remember nothing is automatic. Set the shutter speed, fast for an action shot, slower for most

Hill Williams Jr. stands in the sand to capture a photo with his Speed Graphic camera. *Author photo.*

pictures. Adjust the lens opening considering both the shutter speed and available light. If you have a light meter, take a reading. If not, make a good guess. If you need more light, screw in a flash bulb. Estimate distance to the subject, turn a knob to move a mark along the distance scale on the side of the camera, causing the bellows to inch in or out. Pull out the film stop (!!!) and stick it in your back pocket so both hands are free to steady the camera. Cock the shutter. And, finally, press the shutter trigger. Slide the film stop back in place before you pull the film holder out and flip it over for another shot.

It all becomes almost automatic. But if you're not careful you can shoot blank film, make double exposures, get fuzzy images, or fog the film by careless handling of film holders.

Compared to point-and-shoot digital cameras of today, the Speed Graphic sounds clumsy and complicated. But it was a standard tool of newspapers for a long time.

As with any long-used tool, photographers were emotionally attached to their Speed Graphics. Larry Dion of the *Seattle Times* donated his to the Museum of History and Industry in Seattle. When Howard Vallentyne left the *Times* to set up an archery business in Grants Pass, Oregon, he mounted his Speed Graphic in a display case visible as you walked in his store.

Probably my clumsiest use of the Speed Graphic camera was when I interviewed Henry Luce, a co-founder of *Time Magazine*. He was in Richland to visit Hanford and I had arranged to meet him before his tour.

The day didn't begin well. I was late arriving at the Desert Inn. I found him waiting, seated, gazing out a window, drumming his fingers. His traveling companion, a stuffy

Time correspondent whose name I forget, reminded me that "Mr. Luce is accustomed to operating on time." The interview was routine; I asked a few bland questions and Luce responded with bland answers.

As I picked up the big Speed Graphic camera to take his picture, I dropped it and the part that runs on a track to focus the lens came loose. I couldn't get it back on. I asked Mr. Stuffy Correspondent if he knew how to reassemble it and he shook his head and looked out the window. I don't remember if Luce was watching this or had also found something interesting out the window.

I finally held the focusing parts together with my thumb, guessing its position, and flashed the picture. Surprisingly it was usable and ran in that afternoon's paper.

When I told my boss, Don Pugnetti, what had happened, he got laughing so hard he couldn't talk. When he calmed down he told me: "What you should have said was 'Well, Mr. Luce, since I can't take your picture, let's talk about a job for me on *Time* magazine.'"

❧   ❧   ❧

The words I wrote in the *Tri-City Herald* on January 26, 1951, seem unexciting now:

"Incorporation of Richland and sale of government-owned real estate, both residential and commercial, to private interests have been found feasible, the *Tri-City Herald* learned today."

But those words burst like fireworks in a government town where Uncle Sam owned the houses and set the rents, owned the commercial buildings and decided who would run the businesses inside the buildings.

Residents had been on edge for weeks. The Atomic Energy Commission (AEC), whose contractors ran the town as well as the plutonium-producing plants, had hired a consultant to study possibilities for Richland's future. Results were to be announced at a press conference.

There was a lot to wonder and worry about. Would the home rents, which were low, be raised? Would residents get a chance to buy the house they'd lived in for years? Would the operator of a grocery, for instance, be able to stay in the building he was leasing, or buy it?

My story continued: Occupants of houses and commercial leaseholders would get first chance to buy the property. In duplexes, the longest-term resident would get first chance.

Residential rents should be raised...few residents would buy their own homes if payments would be higher than rent.

And it was exciting that Richland, with a population in 1951 of more than 20,000, might be incorporated as a real city rather than a government town with a city council that had only advisory powers.

Living in Richland had been an unusual experience since 1943 when Uncle Sam condemned homes and stores in the village of 250 or so residents and built a town for Hanford workers.

If your house needed painting, a government worker decided the color, not always the choice of the occupant. And the government hired the painter. Plumbing problem? Well, it was government property so a government employee would come to the house and fix it. And there were those low rents, although an increase had been proposed. Residents in neighboring cities thought Richlanders were pampered.

It was going to be a big story. The AEC, chronically irked at the *Tri-City Herald*'s aggressive coverage, had scheduled an afternoon press conference on January 25, 1951. The timing meant our competition at the time, the short-lived *Columbia Basin News* published each morning in Pasco, would beat us on the story. We were an afternoon paper, and the *News,* a morning paper, would use the story the next morning. The *Tri-City Herald,* an afternoon paper, wouldn't be on the street or delivered to homes until that afternoon.

I managed to obtain a copy of the report the day before the press conference, and stayed up all night to read it and prepare stories. As we left the press conference the next afternoon, we passed a newspaper box that displayed my stories with a two-line headline eight columns wide:

INCORPORATION OF RICHLAND IS GIVEN

GREEN LIGHT BY CONSULTANTS FOR AEC

But the strangest part of the story in this unusual town happened that night. Officials from the AEC and the General Electric Co., AEC's prime contractor at that time for both the town and Hanford plants, visited the homes of everyone who had received an advance copy of the report and asked to see it—an attempt to identify the leaker. The visitors included David Shaw, AEC general manager at Hanford.

It illustrated the agency's continued obsession with secrecy—almost six years after the end of World War II, two years after the Soviet Union had detonated its own plutonium bomb—about a report that had nothing to do with plutonium production.

I had returned the borrowed report before the press conference. As far as I know, the leaker was never identified.

In 1958 Richland voted to be incorporated as a first-class city with a population of 22,970, the state's 11th largest city at that time.

❖   ❖   ❖

This was a long time ago, maybe the 1960s. The trial in Sno-homish County Superior Court involved the kidnapping of a young boy, 10 or 12 years old, and a demand for ransom.

Testimony revealed how much smarter the kid was than his kidnapper. He made impossible demands, sent the kid-napper on useless errands and ultimately escaped easily.

The testimony reminded me of the 1907 short story by O. Henry, "The Ransom of Red Chief," where two men kid-napped the red-headed son of a prominent businessman and demanded ransom. The family refused. The boy, who called himself Red Chief, drove his kidnappers to distraction, talking constantly and giving orders. They reduced the ran-som several times which the family continued to refuse. The kidnappers finally paid the family to take the kid back.

Well, it didn't go that far in the kidnapping case I was cov-ering, but there were similarities. I wrote stories each day that emphasized how the kid dominated his captor—good, readable and funny stories.

But after a couple of days, the boy's parents approached me during a court recess. They said the stories were accurate, readable, even funny. But, they added, "they didn't tell what we were going through."

The parents were right. They were good stories. But they would have been better if they had incorporated the terror of parents with a missing child.

It was a good lesson for a young reporter.

Seattle and the *Times*

WHEN I MOVED TO SEATTLE to work at the *Seattle Times* in 1952 I didn't even consider an apartment where I'd have to do my own cleaning and cooking. For a single guy, boarding houses seemed the answer. They included a furnished room, meals, someone to make the bed and clean the room.

In those days, the "boarding houses" section in newspaper classified ads had many offerings. I quickly found one on Capitol Hill within walking distance of the *Times*.

Mrs. Brown, a tough, likable old gal, rented five rooms to working guys. From my room, I could hear foghorns on Elliott Bay. I liked that. After I'd been there a while, Bill Plunkett, the *Times* police reporter, moved in on my recommendation.

I paid Mrs. Brown $19 a week. She provided breakfast as we left for work on different schedules but we all, including Mrs. Brown, sat together for dinner. There were no lunches or weekend meals. She was a good cook. I had been there about a year when she sold the place. We kept in touch for years.

I moved to another boarding house on Capitol Hill, still walking distance to the *Times*. My room was on the second floor with a view to the Cascade Range where I was pretty sure I could see the gap leading to home in eastern Washington.

The bathroom was on the same floor—bathtub, no showers in those days—but there was a washbowl in my room that seemed a luxury. The rent was $85 a month.

The landlady, Mrs. Kinney, a widow, was a gracious person—dignified, friendly, thoughtful. I was happy there, probably would be there still except Mrs. Kinney retired in June of 1956 and sold the house. She moved to Bayview Manor and occasionally would write me at the *Times* commenting on what I was doing. I sent her our family Christmas pictures over the years and when she died, her daughter-in-law mailed back to us the whole stack of pictures Mrs. Kinney had saved! It touched me.

The next move was to a place on top of Queen Anne Hill, a brisker but still enjoyable walk to work. As Johnny Reddin, a *Times* columnist, drove home from work, he would see me walking up Taylor Avenue and comment the next day, "You were well lathered."

I left the Queen Anne boarding house in November 1957, to share an apartment on Capitol Hill with Howard Brewer, an old friend who was getting out of the Navy.

Looking back, it was a lucky move. The apartment was only a block or so from the apartment of a young lady named Mary Louise Corbett who, two years later, would become Mrs. Mary Louise Williams.

I wonder why young single people no longer live in boarding houses. Has fast food lessened the drudgery of cooking that turned me off? Or are young people more sophisticated than I was? Well, boarding houses weren't fancy but most of them were good, pleasant places to live.

❧   ❧   ❧

I went to work at the *Seattle Times* in 1952 when printers made up pages with lead type and the composing room was filled with clattering Linotype machines.

Write out "etaoin shrdlu" and show it to anyone younger than 60 or so and you'll get a blank stare. But a person who's spent some time around newspaper composing rooms might smile nostalgically and murmur, "I remember. Hot type, lead slugs."

Etaoin shrdlu dates back to the time when lines of type were cast from molten lead as the text of news stories. They were produced in a marvelously complicated machine, the Linotype. If the Linotype operator made an error as he typed a line, there was no practical way to correct it. Instead, he'd finish out the line as quickly as he could to discard it and begin a replacement.

Why "etaoin shrdlu"? The quickest way to fill out an error line was for the operator to run his fingers down the first two vertical columns on the left side of the keyboard.

This is what the Linotype keyboard looked like. You can see how running your finger down the left column would yield "etaoin," and the next column "shrdlu." The keyboard was arranged with these most frequently used keys at the

Linotype keyboard. *Courtesy wikipedia.org/Linotype_machine*

easiest reach for the operator's left hand. Notice that "x" and "z" were the farthest away.

The black keys were for lower-case letters, the white for capital letters, and the blue keys for punctuation marks, numbers, spaces, etc.

The brass matrices, or molds, that actually formed the type, were in a magazine near the top of the Linotype machine. The magazine contained 90 groups of matrices: for example a group of matrices for "e," another for "t" and so on. The keyboard has 90 keys, one for each group of matrices. When the operator pressed a key, a matrix for that letter slid down into position to begin a line of type. When matrices filled out a line, the operator pressed a lever and molten lead was injected to form a slug. (The slug would be too hot to touch for a minute or two.) Then a metal arm reached down to pick up the matrices and lift them to be replaced in their places in the magazine. To change typefaces, as for an advertisement, the operator lifted the magazine off the back of the Linotype and slid in another one.

It would be up to the proofreader or the printer who assembled the type in a page to spot the error line, discard it, and check the reset line. But enough were missed and appeared in news stories—mystifying and annoying readers—that "etaoin shrdlu" is actually defined in the Oxford English Dictionary. A documentary film about the last issue of the *New York Times* to be printed with the hot-metal process, July 2, 1978, was titled "Farewell, Etaoin Shrdlu."

The *Seattle Times'* big composing room was still full of Linotypes in the 1950s and '60s. If there was a breaking story as deadlines approached, a printer known as the copy cutter would cut apart typed news stories from reporters and distribute short takes to several Linotype operators to speed typesetting. Then the copy cutter would be responsible for assembling the pieces of type in the correct order. The *Times* replaced Linotypes probably in the 1970s as it adopted new printing processes, first offset printing and then digital.

❧   ❧   ❧

Long ago, before cell phones, texting, or tweeting, I walked the beat in Box 13 with a couple of Seattle police patrolmen. "Box 13" was how the police once referred to a six-block chunk of Seattle's Skid Road, extending from the waterfront to Occidental Avenue, between Yesler Way and Jackson Street.

The name came from a police call box, Box 13, at First Avenue South and South Washington Street. You don't see police call boxes any more unless in a museum. But for much of the 1900s they were the link between foot patrolmen and the precinct. Officers checked in on a regular schedule, could call for help or report anything unusual. And if they didn't check in on schedule, someone would go to see why.

It was 1958 when I joined Patrolmen Frank Marshall and Fred Lipke on their eight-hour walking patrol of Box 13. I wrote in the *Seattle Times*:

> The patrolmen wave to bartenders and store operators, giving the establishments a quick look-over as they pass. Marshall, a big man, a 30-year veteran of the police, absently bangs his 18-inch club against parking meters and light standards as he walks. Lipke, 40, a policeman for 16 years, lets his club hang from his belt. They rarely find it necessary to use the clubs on the defeated, aimless men who live in Box 13.
>
> "On a beat like this, you get to know the people and know their troubles," Lipke says. "And lots of times you can help them. I like it."

They stop to talk to a bedraggled old man who is trying not to sway when he saw the blue uniforms. Marshall peers into the unshaven face. "Where do you live?" The derelict mumbled the name of a rundown hotel around the corner. "Well, get on home and sleep it off before you hurt yourself," Marshall ordered.

Marshall muses as we resume walking. "We try to give them a break if we can. These old fellows just have four walls to stare at where they live, nothing to do. You can't blame them for wanting to get out once in a while." Inhabitants of Box 13 know the patrolmen and Marshall and Lipke know most of them. Marshall claims he can spot a newcomer a block away.

Curses and a thump behind them cause the patrolmen to wheel around. Two young men erupt from a tavern and fall, grappling, to the sidewalk. Marshall looks sharply, grins and says: "Well, no knives, anyway." Lipke separates the men, listens to their grievances and sends them off in opposite directions, warning them not to be on the streets again that night. One glances back angrily as he ambles away.

"That guy, the one with the leather cap, hasn't worked a day in years that I know of," Marshall says. "I don't know how he lives. It would drive me crazy."

We enter the open door of a mission dormitory. Marshall uses his club to bang a signal on the wall as we climb to the second floor. "To let them know who's walking in," he tells me. About half the double-decker bunks are occupied by sleeping men. An attendant walks over to talk.

"These beds are free," he tells me, "but you have to attend services to get one. The bunks downstairs are 25 cents a night."

A block away, a second-floor hotel rents sleeping spaces for 52 cents a night, or $3.10 a week. The big room has cubicles separated by partitions halfway to the ceiling. Chicken wire stretched over the partitions covers the cubicles.

Marshall points his club at a shabby tavern on a nearby corner. "That's the lowest," he says. "That's where you see the real human derelicts. I don't know where they sleep or where they get the 15 cents for a glass of wine.

"The next stop is the grave."

☙   ☙   ☙

A couple of bored-looking cows moved out of my way as I climbed through a pasture and up a small knoll near the southwestern Washington town of Raymond. I had heard a strange, sad story about a grave more than a century old and wanted to see it.

There were several dozen graves in a small plot among some trees at the top. One of them, old and weather stained but still legible, said simply: Wm. Kiel, Born Jan. 12, 1836, Died May 19, 1855.

So this was the end of the Oregon Trail for Willie Kiel who made the trip, strange to say, after he had died. My story in the *Seattle Times* in 1969 said that Willie "in death, undoubtedly did more to assure the safe passage of the wagon train over the long and dangerous Oregon Trail than he ever could have if he had lived."

This is how it came about: Willie's father, Dr. William Kiel, was head of a Bethel Christian group in Missouri that was moving to a site, already selected, near Willapa Bay in what is now southwest Washington. Departure date was May 23, 1855. Willie was seriously ill with malaria and he begged his father not to leave him behind.

The departure date couldn't be postponed if the party hoped to get over mountain passes before winter. Dr. Kiel promised Willie he would go and that he would spend Christmas in the new land. But Willie died four days before departure.

Dr. Kiel kept his promise. He built a casket lined with sheet lead, filled it with alcohol and sealed Willie's body inside. One story is that Dr. Kiel used whiskey to fill the casket. That could be true because high-grade whiskey was among the products the group had made and sold in Missouri.

Willie's casket rode in a wagon pulled by two mules at the head of the train. To pass time on the trail, the travelers often got out musical instruments and played and sang hymns. The story spread of "the singing wagon train led by a dead man" and Indians left the group strictly alone even though it was a time when Indians, unhappy at the large numbers of settlers moving on the trail, were increasingly hostile.

The party reached Willapa Bay on November 11 after a surprisingly uneventful trip. Willie spent Christmas in the new land, as his father had promised. He was buried the day after Christmas.

&-   &-   &-

It seems so long ago that we were letting the magnificent Lake Washington deteriorate into a murky, smelly (on warm, sunny days, at least) embarrassment.

This was happening in the late 1950s and early '60s. The lake's water had become so cloudy that, in a standardized test, an eight-inch white disk faded from view at three feet depth. In 1950, the disk had been visible through twelve feet of water.

Floating mats of an algae appeared in quiet bays on warm, sunny days in the early 1960s. Gobs of algae washed up on beaches. Swimmers sometimes emerged wearing a sticky film of algae.

What caused the deterioration? Rapidly growing population after World War II and sewage-treatment plants that discharged their effluent to the lake. It was treated to kill disease-causing bacteria, but not to remove chemicals.

University of Washington scientists, led by zoologist W. Thomas Edmondson, determined that phosphorous was the biggest chemical culprit in the treated sewage effluent, causing an explosive growth of algae.

And in 1958, in a vote hard to imagine today, taxpayers in Lake Washington's drainage basin OK'd formation of the Municipality of Metropolitan Seattle and agreed to pay for diverting treated sewage away from the lake. Edmondson called it "a remarkable public action."

Diversion of effluent away from the lake was completed in 1968. That year, the white disk was again visible at twelve feet depth, with water back to its 1950 clarity.

But the lake surprised everyone, including Edmondson. The water continued to clear as the lake recovered. The disk could be seen at 40 feet depth a few years later. Edmondson said water was the clearest it had been in 35 years.

I wrote in 1984:

> Make no mistake. If you lived within a few miles of Lake Washington in the 1950s and early 1960s, you were part of its problems. And if you have lived in the Lake Washington Basin since 1958, you have helped pay for the lake-rescue effort that attracted scientific attention around the world…

As the first big lake to be rescued after traveling so far down the pollution road, it attracted worldwide scientific attention. Scientists considered the project an outdoor experiment in lake fertilization. Water-quality experts viewed it as an unprecedented rescue of a major lake from premature death.

Since then other lakes have benefited from lessons learned at Lake Washington. Even so, scientists still talk about "the Lake Washington experience."

The lake's recovery coincided with the 1962 publication of Rachel Carson's book, *Silent Spring,* widely credited with helping to awaken the environmental movement. And a massive oil spill off the California coast near Santa Barbara in early 1969, the nation's largest spill to that time, added to concern over the environment. The first Earth Day was April, 22, 1970.

Edmondson—Tommy to almost everyone—died January 10, 2000, at age 84.

❦   ❦   ❦

I was surprised but also intrigued when the *Seattle Times* city editor asked if my wife and I would trade jobs—with her in the newsroom and me at home with the kids—for a week and then write about it.

This was in 1974 when stay-at-home dads were not very common. Mary Lou and I talked about it. She had been a reporter on the newspaper in Yakima before I knew her. And I figured I could survive a week managing things at home. So we agreed to do it.

You may be interested in excerpts from a sort of diary we used in one of the stories:

> **Hill:** I had some second thoughts as the week approached. Would I get so irritable that it would be a hard week on the kids? Could I still read recipes? Would the house get so dirty that Mary Lou would be digging out for weeks?
>
> **Mary Lou:** I was wondering if I could still do a respectable job of reporting after 15 years away? I was a little afraid of

feeling foolish, of being more trouble in the office than I was worth.

I fixed dinner at home that night, washed the dishes and cleaned up the kitchen—for the last time for a week. Had butterflies as after 9 o'clock I removed the graham cracker and plastic pants that I always carry in my purse for the baby and laid out my bus pass for the morning.

I wondered if things went so well at home that I'd lose some of my "status" as a homemaker. Would I miss the children terribly? Would they miss me? Especially Michael, the baby?

Hill: I woke up early the first morning, despite my resolve to let HER wake ME for a change. It was an odd feeling to see her walk out the door at 6:40. I watched her all the way to the corner from a house that seemed awfully quiet.

It was 45 minutes before I had to wake the kids. I looked at the outline of "daily things to do" that Mary Lou had left me. It looked like a busy day but possible if I kept at it. But I was reckoning without the slowing—even paralyzing—effect of a healthy, happy, busy two-year-old in the house.

Mary Lou: Hill had showed me the employee door at the *Times* but I couldn't find it for the longest time. A guard watched me as I tried one door after another. When I did get to my desk, I felt guilty because I didn't have enough to do. At home I always have a backlog of things to do.

The reporters and editors treated me matter-of-factly as though I'd been there all the time. That was nice but it was embarrassing not to know the routine. Once when I asked for a photographer for an assignment, the desk man reared back in his chair and said: "Well, you don't need to be so polite about it!"

I didn't discover the bulletin board with the list of my assignments until about an hour before quitting time. Luckily, I'd done them all.

Hill: I was fixing breakfast for the kids—cold cereal—when Tom, the third grader, asked sarcastically: "What's for dinner, Mom?" with emphasis on the "Mom."

"Meat loaf," I said smugly. Mary, 13, had already found the recipe for me.

Joe, the first grader, "Dad, do you really know how to make meat loaf?" "Wait and see," I responded. He smiled reassuringly: "I'll help you."

It was a shock to open the dirty clothes chute. "Good Lord, look at that." Mary looked. "That's nothing, Daddy."

Mary Lou: I had my first interview on the second day and suddenly it was just like old times, as though I'd never been away from the newspaper business.

One of the desk men said my copy looks better than some of the regulars. I don't know if he really meant it, but I was still thrilled. My confidence was growing.

I had bought a sandwich at the cafeteria and ate it at my desk. Some of the reporters gave me a bad time: "What's the matter? Won't Hill pack you a lunch?"

Things have deteriorated a bit on the home front. I found out today the boys haven't changed shirts for school for three days.

Hill: Who would think they would need reminding to change shirts? And I felt dumb about that lunch bit. I resolved to do better.

I feel more tied to schedules than to deadlines at work. Mike needs to be down for his nap by 1 P.M. If he doesn't nap, life isn't worth living. The roar of homecoming from school at 2:30 wakes him up. By that time, I'm trying to start dinner—and fold laundry from the day before.

Mary Lou: The biggest surprise to me is how quickly I got back in the job routine. As one of the reporters said: "I guess it's sort of like swimming. Once you know how, you just don't forget."

I have no desire to be employed while the children are small, but I think it would be fun to repeat this occasionally. How about you?

Hill: Well, maybe, after a good long rest back at the office.

People

WE WERE IN AN INDIAN STYLE CANOE in the Strait of Juan de Fuca off the mouth of the Hoko River as Harold Ides patiently, meticulously described what it was like when Indians still hunted whales in canoes, armed with hand-thrown harpoons. Cloudy and cool, almost chilly, the day belied mid-August in 1978.

Ides, 80, spoke from first-hand knowledge. He had been on those hunts as a young man.

"We used canoes about this size," he said. (We were in a 32-footer and Ides had scrambled in more nimbly than I). "Except they had more freeboard, were higher on the sides. They could take quite a storm."

As a husky teenager, Ides had manned a paddle in the sea-going canoes. He said they used pointed paddles to reduce splashing or dripping that would warn the whale. Ides remembered that the whale hunter stood in the bow, directing the paddlers with silent signals.

I wrote in the *Seattle Times*:

"When the whale would dive," Ides said, "the hunter would take us to where it would surface. He often knew just where the whale would come up next."

After the kill, they would begin the long, back-breaking trip home to Neah Bay with the paddlers towing the dead whale. One time a steam towboat returning to port after towing a sailing ship out of the strait threw the Indians a line and towed them to the village. Otherwise, it could take days to get back.

Ides was on some of the last of those hunts. He said it would have been around 1914.

Ides was an invaluable help to Washington State University researchers studying ancient villages of the Makah Tribe.

One of the researchers, Dale Croes, said "the depth of Harold's knowledge was very unusual. He was our link to a body of knowledge that was passed down for hundreds of generations."

On another day, I was watching a Seattle television crew preparing to interview Ides about how ancient wooden halibut hooks were baited and used. Croes tried to tell him what to expect during the interview.

"Don't worry. I know what to do," Ides told Croes gently. And he did. In his soft voice, he calmly and lucidly explained use of the old hooks. As the interviewer finished and sang out, "Thank you, Mr. Ides," Harold smiled slyly at some of us who were watching and snapped "Cut!"

I learned later Ides had hunted sea lions as a young man and I wished I had asked him about that. Other members of the Makah Tribe told me that hunters holding torches in their mouths would swim into caves at the base of Cape Flattery's cliffs to kill sea lions and drag them out.

Ides was born in Neah Bay, the son of Jack and Fanny Ides. His father, a proud whale hunter, fisherman, and canoe builder, refused to use the English language, even though the white man had been in the area for decades and Indians, including Jack, had been forced to take Anglicized names.

"He was a brilliant man but it was a matter of pride with him to speak only Makah," John Ides, a grandson of Jack and nephew of Harold Ides, told me.

Harold Ides spoke English fluently and well. But those who knew both languages told me he structured his English in the Makah way.

John Ides, the nephew, called me when Harold died early in 1980. John told me that Harold, 81, had been chopping wood at his Neah Bay home when he suffered an apparent heart attack. He was helped into the house and when he realized he was dying, he told Isabell, his wife of 63 years, goodbye. He used the Makah language.

Isabell, who didn't learn English until her teen years when she was sent away to a boarding school in Tacoma, taught the Makah language and basket-making to hundreds of children. She died in 2001 at the age of 101, one of the few Makah native speakers.

❧   ❧   ❧

Beth Tampien called me at the *Seattle Times* in the summer of 1990. It took me a few seconds to click back to the 1940s and '50s when Beth was writing a column, "The Farmer's Wife," for the *Tri-City Herald*. I was a reporter at the *Herald* at that time.

Beth and her husband, George, an electrician at Hanford, had bought a 65-acre farm along the Yakima River in 1948 and moved from a government-owned house in Richland, still a government town at that time. The farm house had been built by homesteaders in the 1880s—rough-sawed boards held together by square nails. Newspapers insulated the walls. Neither had lived on a farm before.

"I thought it was a crummy house but with a beautiful barn," she said.

Beth walked in to the *Herald* office one day in 1948 to talk to the women's editor about writing something for the paper. The women's editor (newspapers actually had women's editors in those days) was my mother, Ursula Trainor Williams, who herself had grown up on a farm. The result was the column, "The Farmer's Wife," that ran from 1948 to 1959.

Beth was now 81 and living in Bellevue when she called to tell me about a family project that surprisingly had become much bigger. Thinking her family would value tales of life on the farm, she pulled together more than 400 of her columns and had them bound in books for her family—plus one for the Richland Library.

It turned out she had more family than she realized. The copy in the Richland Library really caught people's attention.

So Beth had called to tell me that with help from the Richland Library, and the Mid-Columbia Library in Kennewick, the family volume had been updated and 400 printed for sale.

Thinking about it, maybe it wasn't surprising. The chatty, homespun column appealed to readers in the 1940s and '50s, people who were still thinking about homes, farms, family, and friends they had left behind to take jobs at Hanford during World War II.

Katie Foley, director of the Richland Library in 1990, told me, "A lot of people really related to what she wrote about. It reflected an important part of their lives. People who saw our copy of her book kept asking 'When can I buy a copy'?"

Virginia McKenna of the Mid-Columbia Library told me, "The first thing many people did was to turn to 'The Farmer's Wife' in the Sunday paper to see what the Tampiens were doing. They seemed so much a part of the community."

I wrote about the column in the *Seattle Times* in 1990:

> Readers laughed when George mistakenly sprayed Beth's vegetable garden with herbicide rather than insecticide. They were saddened when someone shot a wild horse that had been running free in the hills above the farm. And they wept when Ann, the Tampiens's 19-year-old daughter, died in 1958…

The time Beth delivered Rufus, a lamb, to the slaughter-house. "I feel like a heel," she wrote. "He trusted me to the last, even when I led him off the scales and into the pen for the overnight stay at the slaughterhouse."

Or the stormy winter night when George laid blankets on the kitchen floor for a newborn calf that was chilling in the barn.

In the last column she told readers that "with less and less of farming, the two litters of pigs about to go to market, the milk cows sold off and only a few scrub beef, hardly enough to keep down the lush pastures, not many chickens and them doing nothing but eating and waiting for spring...

"And now with our girl gone, our oldest son off to the Air Force and only our seventh grader at home, there is little to record."

Beth told me that it had been an extraordinary experience compiling the columns for the book. "I cried a lot inside and sometimes outside. Other columns made me laugh until I cried."

The Tampiens sold the farm in 1964 and moved to a farm in the Cherry Valley near Duvall. George died in 1969 at age 65. Beth lived in a condo in Bellevue when she called. She was taking care of a patio yard.

I quoted her: "It's only 10 by 20 feet but in one end of it I have a vegetable garden. No one else in the complex plants tomatoes and carrots. And in the winter I have a compost heap."

Beth died in 2004 at age 95.

☙   ☙   ☙

I first heard of this man....well, no, that's not quite right. Actually, I first heard of one of his surprising projects: the astounding creation of a salmon run that returned to the University of Washington campus each spawning season.

These homebound fish, back from years at sea, entered Seattle at Shilshole and passed under a railroad bridge (possibly with a train roaring across), struggled upstream in a fish ladder to gain 20 feet from sea water to lake water at Ballard Locks, swam on in the Ship Canal, under the low Ballard and Fremont Bridges, the high Aurora Bridge and the even higher Freeway Bridge, unerringly crossed busy Lake Union to find the Montlake Cut and finally their instinctive spawning grounds.

From the Pacific Ocean to the university, the salmon had followed the distinctive odor of the water in which they were hatched. In nature it would be the gravelly bottom of a stream. Here their instinctive home water was pouring down a fish ladder leading to concrete-lined ponds behind the U.W. Medical Center. It wasn't city water with its chlorine and other additives, but water pumped from the Montlake Cut, the salmon's home water.

Denied the dignity of spawning in a stream, the salmon were grabbed and killed by students and faculty, the male fish stripped of milt and the females of eggs to be nurtured and hatched in School of Fisheries laboratories for the next season's release of fingerlings.

The man who created this unlikely tribe of salmon was happiest during the annual run, usually in the thick of it manhandling the big fish and helping students. Dr. Lauren R. Donaldson, professor of fisheries, had established the run in 1949, a follow-up to an assignment during World War II. His wartime work had involved testing Columbia River salmon for effects of radioactive discharges from Hanford nuclear plants.

Unfortunately, for me anyway, the university decided that 2010 would be the last release of young fish because of budget cuts and "new directions in aquatic research." The returning fish in 2014 ended it except for a few stragglers in later years that didn't find the fish ladder with its beckoning water.

Over the years Donaldson (Doc to almost everyone) selectively bred salmon and trout for quicker growth, increased size, and egg production. His lab provided salmon eggs that grew into thriving fisheries in the Great Lakes as well as half a dozen foreign countries.

Doc was awarded the first annual National Sea Grant College Award in 1971 and was named the University of Washington Alumnus Summa Laude Dignatus, the highest award the university can bestow.

Yet when he was retiring in 1973 and I asked what he considered his greatest accomplishment, he jumped out of his chair and walked to a bookshelf. He stretched his arms as far as they would reach and barely encompassed a row of black-bound volumes.

"These," he said, "These are my greatest accomplishment. My students."

Then he read the names of the students on the spines of the doctoral and master's theses—and told me where most of them were and what they were doing.

Doc died in 1998 at age 95.

❧   ❧   ❧

Leonhard Seppala was a small, trim man. He spoke quietly as he answered my questions about his part in a heroic dog-sled run delivering serum to a Nome stricken with an outbreak of diphtheria in 1925. The Great Race of Mercy, as the media called it, caught the world's attention. But like most big stories it had largely faded from memory in the 40 or so years that had passed when we spoke.

Diphtheria was spreading in Nome, the needed serum was in Anchorage. It was Alaska's coldest winter in 20 years and the only practical way to deliver the serum was by dog sled from the railroad's northernmost point to Nome, a run of 670 miles. The plan was for other mushers to carry the serum part of the way, meeting Seppala, 48, who would drive his dog team south from Nome to pick up the medicine and rush it back.

Seppala's round trip was about 400 miles and it included dangerous crossings—both ways—over the treacherous ice of Norton Sound. A storm blew in on his return trip with winds of 70 miles an hour and a wind chill approaching minus 100 degrees Fahrenheit.

After four days on the trail, back and forth, Seppala passed the serum to another relay musher, now only about 70 miles from Nome. The precious medicine was in Nome, thawed and in use on February 2, 1925, five days after Seppala began the trip.

Seppala credited his lead sled dog, Togo, 12 years old, for helping find the way through the tumbled ice on Norton Sound. But, to his dismay, Balto, the lead dog on the team that finished the final miles to Nome, got most of the publicity. A statue of Balto was placed in New York City's Central Park only 10 months after the run.

Nevertheless, Seppala and the dog team led by Togo drew crowds in a tour of the country from Seattle to Washington, D.C. In New York Seppala drove the team from the steps of City Hall along Fifth Avenue and through Central Park. Togo died in 1929 at 16 years. He was eulogized in several newspapers, including the the New York *Sun Times* with the

Leonhard Seppala. *Courtesy Carrie M. McLain Memorial Museum, Nome, Alaska.*

headline "Dog Hero Rides to His Death." Seppala had Togo custom mounted for display in a museum in Alaska.

Alaska's annual Iditarod Race is a reminder of the Great Race of Mercy, mostly following the same route to Nome, but longer.

Seppala, 89, died in Seattle on January 28, 1967, 42 years to the day after he began the famous run. He is buried in Nome.

❧   ❧   ❧

Harold McCluskey in 1977.
Courtesy www.aol.com. AP Photo.

I talked to Harold McCluskey about four years after he had suffered the biggest internal dose of radiation of any surviving nuclear worker in history. In fact, his dose was more than the total known internal exposures of all radiation workers in the world up to that time, from the beginning of the Atomic Age.

"Obviously, it was the biggest dose I'd ever seen," said Dr. Bryce Breitenstein, the Hanford physician who directed McCluskey's treatment. "I don't think there had even been animal experiments with internal levels this high."

McCluskey was not what you would call a well man when Roy Scully, Seattle *Times* photographer, and I visited him at his home near Prosser. But he was home after months of treatment. And he was defiantly upbeat.

"When I hired on," he told us with a half grin, "the man doing the orientation was telling us the pros and cons of nuclear work. He held up a pin and said that as much radioactive material as would fit on the head of a pin could kill you. Well, you'd need a wagon for what I took in."

McCluskey was injured in a laboratory explosion August 29, 1976, while at work at Hanford. He was separating americium from nuclear waste, working behind a leaded-glass window. Americium, a radioactive product of nuclear reactions, is useful in research and the manufacture of electronic products.

A chemical—not nuclear—explosion blew americium, nitric acid, and shattered glass into the right side of

McCluskey's face and body. He was 65 at the time, planning to retire in a few months.

By the time I met him, 95 percent of the radioactive material deposited on and in his body had been removed. Much of the treatment was low tech—scrubbing, scrubbing, and scrubbing. But Dr. Breitenstein's team also used a drug known as DTPA which had shown promise elsewhere in animal experiments in reducing internal radioactive contamination. The drug attracts heavy metals such as americium and aids in their excretion from the body, principally in urine.

McCluskey had had six hundred DTPA shots by the time we talked, ten times the amount any human had had previously. No drug-related problems had developed.

Dr. Breitenstein said McCluskey had not developed any ailments that could be definitely blamed on the radiation. But there were three conditions where he said radiation must be considered a strong possible cause.

- Cataracts developed on both eyes but did not show expected characteristics of radiation-induced cataracts. They were removed and his eyesight improved to where he could pass the vision test for a driver's license.
- An explosion wound near his right eye had been strangely slow to heal. But it was also hard hit by nitric acid and bits of shattered glass. "We can explain it on the basis of the acid, but there could have been some radiation effect." Dr. Breitenstein said.
- There was a decrease in the platelet count in McCluskey's blood, not alarming but below normal for a man McCluskey's age. Platelets are formed in the bone marrow. Much of his permanent deposition of americium was in the bone where it would irradiate the marrow for the rest of his life.

"We can't say for sure the platelet level is due to the americium, but it has to be a major consideration," Dr. Breitenstein said.

McCluskey had a small radiation detector at home. It clicked occasionally from normal background radiation as we talked. But the clicking picked up when he ran it over a spot on his right shin and just above the knee, marking concentrations of americium in the bone.

And the clicking sounded like severe radio static as he held it to his lower right jaw. "Here's the hottest spot, right here," he said. "It's not near as bad as it was."

Although McCluskey never returned to work, he became known among Hanford workers as the Atomic Man, with some justification. After all, he was the most radioactive man in the world.

An investigation revealed the chemical mix that exploded had been stored longer than it should have been. The government awarded McCluskey $275,000 in 1977.

McCluskey died in 1987 at age 75 of coronary artery disease, ten years after the accident. As far as doctors could tell, he never developed cancer.

Cold War Years

THE COLD WAR, 1947 TO 1991…a time of scary memories. The United States and the Soviet Union, nuclear-armed superpowers held at bay by the idea of mutually assured destruction; the Berlin Blockade in 1948 and 1949; the Soviet Union's brutal crushing of the Hungarian uprising in 1956, and the Prague Spring in 1968; the Cuban Missile Crisis in 1962, the Vietnam War, the Soviet invasion of Afghanistan in 1979.

There were air-raid drills in schools. An alarm horn tested once a week in my town. Some of us considered fixing a corner of the basement as a shelter against radiation from a bomb. American missiles nestled in silos around the country, ready to fire, staffed on a 24-hour basis.

Remember White Alice? It was the nickname for a U.S. Air Force telecommunication network in far-north Alaska during the Cold War, intended for early detection of intercontinental ballistic missiles fired from the Soviet Union. None came and White Alice was eventually replaced by satellite communications.

The Army manned radar stations in the Saddle Mountains across the Columbia River north of the Hanford plutonium plants watching for bombers.

And there were manned anti-aircraft guns in the nuclear reservation itself. When the Hanford Highway across the reservation opened in the 1950s you still passed circles of sandbags that had surrounded the guns. The guns and soldiers were gone, but locust trees the soldiers planted and watered had managed somehow to survive. Even the trees are gone now.

There was a powerful radar installation in North Richland, I discovered to my surprise.

As a *Tri-City Herald* reporter I was driving to an assignment in North Richland, big Speed Graphic camera and a package of flash bulbs on the seat beside me.

There was a flash. It startled me. I checked the car; everything seemed OK. No one outside was running around. I kept driving and a few minutes later, another flash. I wondered, "Could it be?" I checked the flash bulbs. Sure enough, two of them had fired.

I found out later from soldiers stationed in North Richland that if you and a flash bulb were in the right place when the radar beam swept past, the bulb would flash. They sometimes used it for pranks.

A few years later I was covering a scientific meeting in Seattle for the *Seattle Times*. Some geologists from the Soviet Union were there and on a spur-of-the-moment, goodwill gesture, I began the complicated procedure of inviting one of them to our home for dinner. One of our sons, in grade school, was surprised we were having a Communist in the house, an attitude typical of many Americans at the time. "What'll you do if he pulls a gun on you?" he asked me.

As it turned out, the geologist was a really nice guy and probably not a member of the Communist Party. The "guardian," a political officer traveling with the group, was thoroughly unpleasant and he was the one I had to deal with. We set a time for me to pick up him and the geologist downtown. He changed it without telling me and then wondered why I was late. We were doing some remodeling and they had to walk around a sawhorse as they entered our home. He acted as though it was an insult.

But it was a pleasant experience. There was a lot of smiling but little conversation because only the "guardian" spoke English. The geologist, Yuri Sheviakov, gave me a lapel pin inscribed with a geologist's hammer and USSR. He gave the family two LP records of the Leningrad Symphony. We still have them. That day was a happy break in a scary time.

❧   ❧   ❧

They were young, working-age men, maybe two dozen of them, crowding off the plane at Boeing Field in early 1957. Most of them ignored the steps, jumping to the tarmac to get a look at another aircraft roaring down the field.

The plane that had brought them to Seattle was a big, four-engine propeller transport, one of the workhorses of that time. But all these guys wanted to see was that jet roaring for takeoff across the field, a Boeing KC-135 tanker. This was early in the big-jet age and the tanker probably was the first they'd seen. The first KC-135 had flown only months before, August 31, 1956, with the legendary test pilot Tex Johnson at the controls. The first commercial service with Boeing's 707 was still more than a year in the future.

These young men were refugees from Hungary where a few months earlier the Soviet Union had launched a brutal, bloody crackdown on a citizens' uprising. Protests sparked by students had begun on October 23, 1956. The uprising seemed hopeful at first as the Soviets hesitated dealing with it, even as protesters established an independent government. But it suddenly turned into one of the darkest episodes of the Cold War when, at 4:15 A.M. November 4, 1956, Soviet tanks rolled into Budapest. Thousands of Hungarians died as Soviet armor took only a few days to put down the rebellion.

I don't remember why this plane, arriving from a refugee-reception area at Camp Kilmer, New Jersey, carried only men. I had talked to Hungarian families in the preceding month or two who told harrowing stories of escaping the violent repression, some walking to the Austrian border. One father told me he led his family reciting the Rosary as they walked toward freedom.

But the men piling off the plane at Boeing Field that day were young, skilled workers, and work was what they were interested in. I wrote in the *Seattle Times*, "Man after man on the plane told an interpreter: 'I can do anything; any kind of work at all.'" I'm sure they were thinking of building planes like that big jet that had just roared aloft.

Under Hungary's Communist government, many had been forced into jobs they were not trained for. A shoemaker had worked in a tank factory. A locksmith had driven a military truck. A business-machine repairman worked in a foundry.

The refugees arriving in early 1957 had sponsor families waiting for them, mostly Hungarians who had arrived earlier.

One of the Hungarians' sponsors talked at length with the men. He told me later he had feared the worst because these refugees had known nothing but Communist schools.

"They were small boys when the Communists came to my country," he said. "I was expecting strangers but found friends. As far as I could learn, years of Communist indoctrination against their parents and against God had no effect at all. They spoke with great respect of their parents. They believe in God as I do. It was a great surprise to me."

President Eisenhower's administration was under intense political pressure to intervene in the few days of the Soviet suppression of the Hungarian uprising. But he considered the risk too great of triggering a war with the Soviet Union, of pitting two nuclear-armed nations against one another.

In addition, the ongoing Suez Canal crisis was deemed more important and more dangerous. It's surprising to remember how much was going on. Abdul Nasser, Egyptian president, had nationalized the Suez Canal on July 26, 1956, and closed the canal to Israeli shipping. Israel invaded Egypt on October 26, 1956, and France and Great Britain began bombing Cairo the next day. President Eisenhower led peace efforts and the United Nations managed to stop the campaigns. Interestingly, France was then also battling an insurrection in Algeria, then still a French colony, and Great Britain was fighting a Communist-led insurgency in Malaya.

Seattle Mayor Gordon S. Clinton welcomed the refugees arriving at Boeing Field that day. His remarks were translated into Hungarian, phrase by phrase: "America's strength lies in our different peoples. We have welded them together and come up with the United States."

Hungarian surnames have indeed been welded into the community.

❧ ❧ ❧

Above-ground, or atmospheric, nuclear weapons testing by the United States was conducted in late 1940s and 1950s in Nevada and the Marshall Islands in the Pacific. The *Tri-City Herald* assigned me to cover a nuclear test at the Nevada test site in 1952.

It was a warm day and our DC-3 flying over sagebrush-spotted lands of northeastern Oregon was bouncing vigorously. We were enroute from Pendleton to Boise to change planes—to a bigger one that didn't bounce so much, I hoped.

But I forgot the bouncing when I spotted faint markings on the barren land below. It was like a faint trail, visible here, not there. One of the pilots came back to talk. This was 1952 and they did that sometimes in those days.

"You're looking at the Oregon Trail," he told me. "You can still see traces of it in this area."

I was thrilled! The historic Oregon Trail! Ruts cut in the sand by wagon wheels. Oxen straining ahead in their harnesses, grinding hooves, occasional messes in the trail. People plodding along, raising dust. Items accidentally dropped or jiggled out of a wagon, broken wagon parts, perhaps a child's toy—ground into the sand by wagon wheels.

This was one of the places along the 2,000-mile trail where the travel stains of tens of thousands of humans and their animals—and an occasional grave—are still visible.

Here the travelers were on the last leg of the long trek, but still with challenges ahead. They knew the Blue Mountains, looming on the western horizon, and later the Cascade Range, promised difficult crossings. Some were considering trading the hardships of the mountains for the hazards of passage on the still-untamed Columbia River.

Traffic was heaviest on the trail in the 20 or so years after 1846 as the lure of free land and a new life in the Oregon country drew farmers, miners, businessmen—many with their families.

But completion of the transcontinental railroad linking San Francisco Bay to the nation's rail network in 1869 pretty much put the Oregon Trail out of business. Now, almost a century later, I looked down on the trail. Rain and snow had erased much of the stains of human travel. Sand had blown over some of the ruts. But here on a sunny day in a low-flying plane over Oregon's desert you could still spot traces of

Press cameras set up at the Nevada test site. *Author photo.*

the trail, marking of one of the great human migrations in history.

A couple of days later I was sitting on a rocky outcrop under a bright mid-morning sun in the Nevada desert, waiting for an atomic bomb to explode. The Atomic Energy Commission had been testing nuclear devices at the Nevada site for some time, but this was the first witnessed by representatives of the nation's media—about 200 of us representing newspapers, magazines, radio, newsreel and television.

The bomb dropped from a B-29 at 30,000 feet was to explode at 3,000 feet—ten miles away from us. I had chosen to watch the explosion through dense, welder's type goggles. Others faced away.

Precisely as the countdown reached zero, a dazzling bright flash caused me to squint, even inside the dark goggles. A startling, even frightening, blast of heat hit us at the same

Hill Williams Jr. stands on News Nob at the Nevada test site. *Author photo.*

instant. Those who had faced away said the sudden light overpowered the sun and threw shadows the wrong way. I yanked off the goggles after a few seconds and grabbed my

Ten miles away the mushroom cloud rises. *Author photo.*

camera. The light was unearthly, unlike sunlight, unlike arti-
ficial light. The ball of flame was transforming to a writhing,
orange-colored cloud, still utterly silent.

About 30 seconds later, a tremendously loud boom reached us, accompanied by a pressure wave that felt as though someone had whacked me on the chest.

We were a quieter bunch as we watched the radioactive cloud, including dust and debris sucked up from the desert floor, drift off to the north and as we began putting together our stories on portable typewriters, the writing tools of that day. It wasn't until later, after deadlines, that I began to absorb the amazing things I'd seen in just a few days.

Peering from an airplane that sped more miles in an hour than the wagons traveled in days, I had seen traces of the Oregon Trail, relic of a massive human migration that had populated much of the continent's western coast.

And I'd seen a light brighter than the sun, a light that changed the world forever, signaling a new era in history.

So what was the most important bit of history I'd seen in those few days in 1952? I still don't know. I'm glad I saw the Oregon Trail. I'm also thankful I've never seen another atomic explosion.

❧   ❧   ❧

From the air, an atoll looks like a necklace thrown carelessly down on the sea so that even though it may be roughly circular there are bends and curves. The dark green islands are bordered on the ocean side by shallow water on the reef, a light, almost fluorescent, green. Surf forms a narrow white band at the outer edge of the reef. Where the reef drops off precipitously is the deep blue of the ocean. On the lagoon side of the islands sandy beaches glare white in the sun as water shelves gradually deepen, changing from a yellowish green to darker green to blue.

The crater in Eniwetak Atoll. *Author photo.*

This was Eniwetak Atoll in the Marshall Islands in the West Central Pacific Ocean in August 1964. I was working with a University of Washington laboratory that was under contract to the Atomic Energy Commission to study recovery at Eniwetak and Bikini Atolls from more than 50 nuclear tests from 1946 to 1958.

Part of the way around the atoll, we flew over a dark blue opening in the reef that looked out-of-place. It separated two islands in the string and made an incongruous gap. The pilot pointed at it and shouted: "That was an island before they blew it up." The blue gap in the reef was the site of America's (and the world's) first test of a hydrogen bomb, a 1952 shot dubbed Mike.

The atoll was evacuated of scientists and construction workers for the test because no one knew exactly what would happen. They waited it out on ships lying 30 miles outside the atoll. The natives had been moved out a year or so earlier. When Mike went off, it was the biggest explosion humans had ever witnessed. The boiling fireball shot up through a cloud layer to reach 130,000 feet in 15 minutes. Where the tiny island had been was a crater a mile wide and 200 feet deep. In a fraction of a second, a reef that had been building for millions of years was severed, the island converted to a fine, white powder that was still drifting with the tide when we swam in the lagoon in 1964.

I opened a window to photograph the gap in the reef. As far as I remember, I was unmoved by the sight except to marvel at the power of the blast to eliminate an island. It still hadn't hit home to me that people had once lived on the atoll and that someone had owned that island.

But it did hit me—hit me hard—in the next few years as I talked to the people who had lived on the Eniwetak and Bikini Atolls in the Marshall Islands. They had left their ancestral homes at the request of the United States to make way for tests of the new atomic bombs. The tests began in 1946 and continued for 12 years.

Not all of those people are home even after all these years.

Johannes was a leader of the Eniwetak people when Navy officers told them that America needed their atoll and they would be moved. Johannes and I happened to be on the same atoll in 1968 and I recruited a Peace Corpsman as interpreter. Johannes was 65 when I met him.

"We didn't understand what was happening," Johannes told me. "We had no idea why they needed Eniwetak. They said we would be given a new island."

The Navy took Johannes to see the promised new island. He remembered that when they got there he told the officers: "This is no new island. We know this place. It is Ujelang.

Ujelang Atoll was uninhabited, for good reason—too small to support people. It had one quarter of the land area and one-fifteenth the size of Eniwetak's lagoon which the people depended on for fish. The people quickly became dependent on supplies from the outside.

Juda was the Bikini leader in 1946 who agreed to lead his people to another island when a U.S. Navy admiral told him America needed their home islands for tests that would benefit all of mankind.

Some anthropologists who had studied the Marshallese people questioned whether the residents of Eniwetak and Bikini understood what they were agreeing to. But it was the mighty United States making the request, the country that had liberated the islands from the Japanese only a year or so earlier. Gratitude undoubtedly was part of it. And, perhaps surprising to us, it would have been foreign to Marshallese culture to turn down a request for cooperation.

So the Bikini people moved to Kili Island, an island lacking the spaciousness of an atoll and lacking a lagoon with the fishing the people depended on.

In 1968, scientists thought radioactivity at Bikini had decreased enough to allow the people to move home. But a trial resettlement failed as it became apparent radioactivity still exceeded safe levels.

The people were still on Kili Island in 1968 when I visited. Juda had died just months before at age 73. I walked to his grave, just down a path from the village. His favorite chair and tea kettle were beside the grave. The tools used to clear the grave site had been thrown in the underbrush, never to be used again, an honor to the leader.

Juda's request as he was dying was that he be reburied at Bikini when possible. It still hasn't happened.

I visited Rongelap, an atoll in the Marshall Islands in the Western Pacific Ocean in 1968 with a scientific group studying effects of nuclear testing. Rongelap village had been accidentally dusted with radioactive fallout from an American test in 1954.

As we waded ashore from our small boat we were greeted by happy, smiling kids, the girls in long dresses, the boys in shorts. I've wondered since if one of the boys who clustered around us was Lekoj Anjain, who would have been about ten.

Lekoj was one year old when his village was hit by fallout from the explosion of a hydrogen bomb at the Bikini testing ground, about 75 miles from Rongelap. The explosion still ranks as the most powerful explosion in history. It was more than 1,000 times more powerful than the bombs dropped on Japan, and apparently twice the energy yield expected by American scientists.

The Rongelap people had been moved to other islands for three years after the accidental dusting and had been back seven years when I visited. But eight years after my visit an

American physician diagnosed Lekoj with leukemia, a common result of radiation exposure to young children. Lekoj was taken to America for treatment but developed pneumonia and died a few months later at age 19.

I wrote in the *Seattle Times* on November 23, 1972:

> I know the tiny cemetery where they'll be burying Lekoj Anjain in a few days…The cemetery is in the middle of the village which is strung out along the beach. It is neatly kept and views of the lagoon are framed by graceful coconut trees.
>
> It's beside the point that Lekoj didn't actually die of leukemia. He still had the tragic distinction of being the world's first known victim of H-bomb fallout to develop leukemia.
>
> Lekoj's family and their neighbors in their peaceful island homes have one thing to be thankful for. We're not shooting off any more of those things at Bikini.

It's been many years since, without emotion, I looked down at a blue hole in the Eniwetak Atoll reef.

My outlook has changed.

❧   ❧   ❧

We were a scruffy looking bunch in August of 1964 as the big Air Force transports, one after the other, landed on the narrow coral strip on Eniwetak, an atoll in the west central Pacific Ocean. Maybe that was why the young, neatly uniformed soldiers seemed cautious when we tried to talk to them.

I was with a University of Washington scientific group assessing the effects of American nuclear testing at the atoll between 1946 and 1958. We had been there long enough to need shaves, haircuts, a laundry.

The hulking C-130 transports were stopping to refuel at Eniwetak on the long hop across the ocean. We didn't know where they were going—and didn't find out when we asked. The soldiers didn't look happy.

As it turned out, their destination was Vietnam, the American reaction to the Gulf of Tonkin Incident. If I had guessed their destination, I would have been as unhappy as they appeared.

I didn't learn until later the events of the night of August 2, 1964, in the Gulf of Tonkin off the North Vietnam coast. The American Navy destroyer *Maddox* radioed that it had evaded an attack by three Vietnam torpedo boats and had opened fire with its 5-inch guns. The nearby aircraft carrier *Ticonderoga* launched four F-8 planes that attacked the retiring torpedo boats, claiming one sunk and one damaged.

Damage to the *Maddox* was minor. It was struck by one machine-gun bullet. The Vietnamese claimed they had hit the *Maddox* with a torpedo and shot down one of the planes.

The destroyer was inside the 12-mile limit claimed by North Vietnam, but not recognized by the United States. There was no agreement on who had fired the first shot. The *Maddox* had fired warning shots as the boats approached, before opening fire.

The media jumped on the story. Several factors increased interest. The Soviet Union was aiding Communist North Vietnam. And there was the Cold War policy of containment, the idea that one country falling to communist forces would lead to others falling like dominoes. The Department of Defense had been sending limited numbers of troops to help train South Vietnam forces.

Two days later, August 4, the *Maddox* and another destroyer, the *Turner Joy*, on an intelligence-gathering patrol in rough weather off North Vietnam, radioed they were under attack again. President Lyndon B. Johnson went on the air that night reporting the second attack and requesting authority for a military response.

As it turned out, there probably was not a second attack. Later examinations of electronic records and interviews indicated the ships were likely firing at false radar images caused by the fierce storm—probably combined with nervousness.

So it was later in August 1964, maybe several weeks after the Gulf of Tonkin Incident, that our scruffy group on an isolated atoll in the western Pacific saw the young soldiers stretching their legs as their planes refueled.

We didn't know, and they wouldn't have either, that they were the beginning of a massive buildup of American troops in Vietnam, early arrivals in the most divisive war the United States has ever fought.

Geology

I WROTE IN THE *SEATTLE TIMES* IN 1971:

It isn't often you live through a genuine scientific revolution, a major overturning of basic principles. But you have if you're old enough to be reading this. It has been a change in geological sciences as stunning as the one Darwin caused in biology, or Copernicus in astronomy with his idea that the sun, not the earth, is the center of the solar system.

The change, of course, has been the sudden acceptance—sudden by scientific standards—of the idea that the continents are drifting imperceptibly.

I felt then, still do, that as science-news writer I had the best job on the newspaper during those years of absolutely stunning changes in ideas on how our corner of North America was put together. Textbooks were being rewritten, professors changing lectures. I was fascinated.

We were learning that in the Pacific Northwest we live in the zone where two of the massive segments of the earth's surface collide. Some of us live on the leading edge of the ancient North American Plate that is creeping west and is actually riding over an ocean-bottom plate that is creeping east.

The rest of us live on later arriving (later as in millions of years) additions to the North American Plate, material scraped off ocean bottom as the eastbound Juan de Fuca Plate thrusts under the ancient continent.

In one of my learning years I was on Kamiak Butte with Peter Hooper, a Washington State University geology professor. Kamiak Butte is a mass of rock that seems out of place looming above the rolling Palouse hills a few miles north of Pullman.

Hooper whacked open a rock with his hammer. The fresh fracture was coarse-grained and whitish.

"That rock was once sand from an ocean beach," he said. "Where we're standing is the western edge of the ancient North American continent. Everything west of here is younger and came from someplace else."

I looked west at a few miles of Palouse Hills. Beyond was desert, the Cascade Range, rain-soaked forest and, more than 300 miles farther, today's coastline where storm-tossed waves were crashing against rocks.

I looked east into Idaho.

So what Hooper was saying was that almost all of Washington State except a narrow strip along the Idaho border is made up of "late arrivals" to the original continent of North America.

❖   ❖   ❖

The story begins about 500 million years ago when the western part of the North American continent was flat and relatively featureless. Streams carried sediment into the ocean, building up beaches, some of which was compressed into rock that make up features like Kamiak Butte.

Then somewhere around 200 million years ago, for reasons that scientists can only speculate about, a vast conveyor-belt system kicked into gear. Parts of distant continents and ocean-bottom bedrock began drifting ever so slowly northeast across the Pacific Ocean toward what is now the Pacific Northwest.

The forces involved were tremendous, with the muscle of the earth behind them. Land masses arriving off the coast crunched into the core continent, tipping, overturning or even shattering older formations of rock. The collisions were so violent that only a few traces of the old coast, such as Kamiak, remain accessible to geologists.

It sounds spectacular and in the long view, it was. But it happened at a rate that would make glaciers seem speedy. The new arrivals moved only one or two inches a year.

Humans were not on earth that long ago but even if they had been, they would not have been aware of what was going on. At two inches a year, it would take more than 30,000 years—1,500 human generations—for an offshore island to drift a mile. Occasional earthquakes as the earth masses jostled each other probably would have been the only noticeable signs.

That long-distance conveyor system building America's western edge shut down about 50 million years ago, again for reasons as obscure as those that started it. And a shorter-range conveyor system went into operation, still powerful and violent, lacking only the drama of the long-range transport.

❧   ❧   ❧

On another day I visited Sackit Canyon near the Canadian border in the northeast corner of Washington State. It's a place where the ice age did scientists a favor, and then took it back.

The creeping ice that scooped out Sackit Canyon bulldozed away younger rocks that hid the predicted boundary of the old and new. Unfortunately, as the ice melted, it left a deposit of its own on top of everything else.

"Almost everyone agrees that east of Sackit Canyon is ancient North America," Robert Powell of the U.S. Geological Survey had told me. He motioned in his small office in Spokane, "Over the width of this room is a glacial deposit that has beneath it the actual contact."

Sackit Canyon is north of Kamiak Butte on the edge of the strip of ancient North America along the Washington-Idaho border.

❧   ❧   ❧

I was with Weldon W. Rau on the Washington State ocean beach a few miles north of Kalaloch as we walked over steeply tilted rock layers, looking something like boards stacked on edge.

Rau, an Olympia geologist, had by that time published maps and two books explaining the formation of today's coastline.

The rock layers, Rau said, were composed of mud, sand, silt and gravel that once had been carried off the continent by streams and laid down in thick deposits on the sloping continental shelf.

Over millions of years, Rau said, the deposits were occasionally shaken by earthquakes that loosened the steeply sloping materials and triggered massive undersea avalanches. Huge clouds of the sediments would be temporarily suspended in the water, finally settling farther down the slope of the continental shelf.

Rau knelt on the tilted rock layers to examine them closely.

"We know that when these huge clouds settled to the bottom," he said, "the coarsest pebbles would settle out first, then the sands and finally, on top, the silt. But if you look closely, you'll see that the coarsest material is on top. That means that these layers have not only been tipped up from their original horizontal position but have actually been overturned."

It was silent evidence of the awesome forces exerted along the coastline for millions of years.

☙   ☙   ☙

As my learning continued, I wrote this for the *Seattle Times* in 1971:

> Someone passed the word: A core is coming up! We hurried to the forward part of the big ship below a drilling derrick towering 200 feet above the sea.
>
> Two roughnecks—they call them by the oil-field term even here on the ship—were wrestling a 31-foot pipe to the deck. Scientists gently slid the plastic-enclosed core of greenish mud from the pipe and laid it on the deck for first observations.
>
> "It took the Columbia River about 10,000 years to lay down that 9½ meters of sediment," said Dr. Lavern D. Kulm of Oregon State University, one of the chief scientists aboard.
>
> I was aboard the *Glomar Challenger*, a deep-sea drilling ship, about 90 miles west of the central Oregon coast.
>
> A paleontologist had smeared a little mud on a slide and ran—yes, he actually ran—for the microscope in his laboratory several decks below to determine the age of the core that had been drilled from 1,600 feet below the ocean floor. I was impressed. The drill had reached through 10,000 feet of water and 1,600 feet of seabed. We examined, touched and smelled the mud as we waited to learn how old it was.
>
> A telephone jangled. The core was about 2 million years old! Long, long before anything resembling modern humans walked the earth. But the Columbia River had been here, doing what it does today, carrying sand, mud, bits of rock and skeletons of marine animals—clues that date the sediment—to the ocean.

The *Glomar Challenger,* a 400-foot ship built exclusively for marine research, represented one of the most exciting science projects ever, probably equal in importance to the Apollo moon project if less well known and much less expensive. Its 15-year career, beginning in 1968, roaming the world's oceans was funded by the National Science Foundation at a time when the United States was more willing to finance pure research.

Interestingly, it provoked the same questions in some minds as had the Apollo moon program: Is man trespassing forbidden territory by walking on the moon or reaching deep within the earth for information predating the dinosaurs?

In the years before I boarded the ship off the Oregon coast it had drilled through water as deep as 20,000 feet and more than 3,200 feet of the seabed, bringing up sediments 180 million years old. All were world records at the time because it was the first ship to roam the earth for the sole purpose of drilling the ocean floor for scientific knowledge.

They were exciting years. Work made possible by the *Glomar Challenger* had absolutely turned upside down the study of earth sciences with the realization that continents were actually moving, carried by creeping seafloor replenished by vents spewing molten rock to form new ocean bottom. The term "plate tectonics" was new to most of us. Here in the Pacific Northwest, we were realizing that a vent off our coast was creating new ocean bottom and pushing it under the edge of the North American continent that, in turn, was creeping to the west over the ocean bottom.

Only a few years earlier in January of 1968, I had written in a *Times* story about the still new idea of plate tectonics that "the rate of movement of continents, if there is movement—and many scientists think there is—is far too slow to measure." I quoted a scientist musing "Just think. If we're on the right track, it means the Atlantic Ocean is almost 40 feet wider now than when Columbus sailed across. I wonder if he would have made another 40 feet."

Well, the cruises of the *Glomar Challenger* helped prove that the continents do move, the movement can be measured and the Atlantic Ocean is about 40 feet wider than it was when Columbus crossed it. And that we in the Pacific Northwest live in one of the most complex and interesting parts of the world, a place where the seafloor and continent are bumping each other.

As we were leaving the ship, one of the roughnecks, Charles McNiel, took me aside. "I have a boy back home in Texas—he's 14—keeping a scrapbook on this program," he said. "Could you send him a clipping or a picture?"

I took the boy's name and the address in Livingston, Texas. That 14-year-old would be middle-aged by now. I hope my story kept him interested in science.

❧   ❧   ❧

If you're a little relaxed and the sun is low, the fertile Palouse Hills of eastern Washington look much like smooth ocean swells. Actually, that wouldn't be too far off. The same wind that piles up ocean waves built the rolling Palouse Hills and helped create the world-famous Palouse soil.

I wrote in 1981:

If you imagine a layer of dust up to 200 feet thick, you have an idea of how the Palouse soil of Eastern Washington was formed.

The thought of that much dust is staggering. But, geologists point out, given a million years, even the frequency and severity of the dust storms that still occur in Eastern

The rolling Palouse Hills. *Photo courtesy of Caryn Lawton.*

Washington would have been sufficient to build up such a layer.

The story of that remarkable layer of soil involves an ice age, the heaving up of a mountain range, a huge lake covering what is now desert and, finally, tens of thousands of swirling dust storms, interspersed with falls of ash from distant volcanoes.

There is not much question that wind action built the Palouse Hills. But some questions still baffle scientists.

For example: Why, especially in the southwestern portion of the two million acres of Palouse country, are the hills lined up precisely 30 degrees east of due north, almost as though laid out by a surveyor.

The story of the Palouse soil goes back a million years. In those times, it was a barren, mostly level place. The surface was basalt, a lava that had poured from huge fissures in the ground millions of years before. Not much soil had accumulated atop the basalt during those millions of years because the Cascade Range had not yet risen and there was nothing to keep moist clouds from the Pacific Ocean from bringing rain to the interior. It eroded any soil.

But the situation had changed by one million years ago. The Cascades had pushed up, cutting off moisture from the ocean and creating a dry, dusty desert. As the Cascades rose, the Columbia Basin tilted toward the southwest with a low spot in the Pasco Basin near where today's Columbia and Snake Rivers join.

Streams fed by melting glaciers in the Rocky Mountains and the North Cascades formed a huge lake in the low spot about a million years ago. The Columbia Gorge had not yet been cut and there was no way for the lake to drain. It spread out for 100 miles.

The streams draining into the lake carried a heavy load of finely ground rock from the mountains, the result of glacial erosion. Thick layers of the sediment settled to the lake bottom.

During the lifetime of the lake, hundreds of thousands of years, variations in climate would decrease stream flow, dropping the level of the lake and exposing the fine sediment on the bottom.

The stage was set for massive wind erosion—and the creation of the Palouse soil. Prevailing wind direction then was apparently the same as today, blowing from the southwest toward the northeast.

For thousands of years, the wind moved the ground-up rock back toward the northeast.

By 200,000 years ago or so, the Columbia River had cut through the Cascades and the huge inland lake had disappeared, resulting in even more dry lake bottom for the wind to pick up and swirl toward the northeast.

The Palouse soil is thickest, some 200 feet, near Colfax in Whitman County. That would have been near the center of the "plume" of windblown dust. The wind-deposited layer thins out in the mountains of Idaho to the east and along the western edge of the Columbia Basin of Central Washington.

Why didn't the next dust storm move newly deposited material, some of it as finely ground as flour, out of the Palouse country? The region was rising toward the foothills of the Rockies, resulting in increased moisture. Rain and snow made possible the establishment of the native bunchgrass that once covered much of the West.

The bunchgrass held the soil in place even as the wind blew and more dust fell and also began the process of enriching the top few feet of soil into the rich, organic layer found by the first farmers when they arrived in the late 1880s.

Most geologists believe the "mass movement" of windblown material to the Palouse had ceased long before the first farmers arrived. The reason: The end of the ice age and retreat of glaciers cut off the source of the material in the Pasco Basin.

❧   ❧   ❧

Palouse Falls in Franklin County is spectacular. But it was formed by an even more spectacular event: the greatest flood known to have occurred anytime, anywhere in the world. I'll first discuss the flood, next Palouse Falls.

I wrote in the *Seattle Times*:

Imagine that you could combine more than 1,000 Columbia Rivers, aim at Spokane and then open the faucet wide. That's how the flood was.

It was caused by the sudden failure of an ice dam formed by a glacial lobe blocking a canyon near where Clark Fork River empties into today's Pend Oreille Lake along the Idaho-Montana border. It backed up a lake that covered much of western Montana. The lake's former shorelines on hills show it was 2,000 feet deep at the dam and 950 feet deep at today's Missoula.

The flood was the last in a series extending over hundreds of thousands of years as the ice sheets that had crept over the northern edge of today's Washington State were melting and retreating.

The ice dam appears to have let go all at once sending vast quantities of water and icebergs rushing southwest toward present-day Spokane.

The flood probably did not last more than a week. But in an amazing coincidence, Mount St. Helens erupted five times during the few decades that included the flood. One of the ash falls is embedded in the flood deposits. So geologists who know the dates of the eruptions tell us the great flood occurred about 13,000 years ago.

It left scars on the countryside that are still only partly healed. Pioneers, impressed by the exposed rock and deep, dry coulees, called it the Scablands, not dreaming the parched country had been carved by a flood.

Palouse hills high enough to be above the torrent retained their soil and grow wheat today. Lower areas were scoured to bedrock and are still barren.

So, what about Palouse Falls?

The flood crossed the central part of the state in three giant rivers, some 20 miles wide. The biggest, the one scientists call

Palouse Falls. *Courtesy of Pacific Northwest National Laboratory.*

the Cheney-Palouse Tract, poured directly into the Palouse River which in pre-flood days flowed generally west and emptied into the Columbia River a few miles upstream from present-day Richland.

But the sheer volume of the flood filled the Palouse channel and slopped south over a divide that separated the Palouse from the Snake River. In just a few days the slopover had cut a channel through the basalt, a rock susceptible to erosion because of fracture zones.

There was what must have been a spectacular waterfall into the Snake that quickly eroded its way upstream. All waterfalls have this characteristic, but Palouse Falls was moving miles in a few days.

Suddenly the water stopped coming and the vast glacial lake drained. And Palouse Falls, which had been eroding rapidly upstream, suddenly slowed to the conventional inches-in-a-thousand-years erosion rate.

At 198 feet tall, Palouse Falls is higher than Niagara Falls but a lot narrower. A visit by the back roads is worth the trip.

❧   ❧   ❧

Timberline Camp, the end of the road on the north slope of restless Mount St. Helens was a strange place in early April 1980.

Earthquakes caused by molten rock bumping and cracking its way up inside the mountain would shake snow off tree limbs. Some shakes were strong enough that geologists would grab their instruments to keep them from falling over. Pickup trucks would rock on their springs.

The jagged Goat Rocks, visible occasionally up toward the summit when clouds parted, was moving an astounding five feet a day, pushed out by rising magma in the mountain.

As I talked to the scientists who spent their days there but their nights in safer quarters, the mountain puffed a black cloud that began drifting in our direction. The ash, when it came down, was black, hard and granular, like sand. It fell on my notebook as I wrote, but unlike soot did not leave a smudge when rubbed.

The ash was old, the geologists told me, rock that had remained in the core of the volcano after an ancient eruption. It was ground up and thrown from the crater by steam explosions as melted snow seeped into the mountain and encountered hot rock. So far, about two weeks before the mountain exploded, there had been no evidence of new material in falling ash.

Harry Truman. *Courtesy Richard Waitt.*

Greg Gilbert, a *Seattle Times* photographer, and I had stopped on our way to Timberline that day to talk to Harry Truman, a tough old goat who had refused, despite warnings and even commands, to leave the lodge he had operated for more than 50 years on Spirit Lake.

Truman, 83, was outside shoveling snow, wearing a T-shirt, when we arrived. Truman knew the officers who delivered the evacuation warnings. And he knew most of their fathers.

"They'd be afraid to move me out of here," he said with a grin. "I'd get them all fired."

He felt the earthquakes every day, he told us. For a while he slept in the basement, but had moved back upstairs. He showed us gadgets he'd rigged up in his kitchen that told him which way the ground moved in a quake—east-west or north-south.

I wrote in the *Seattle Times* on May 4, 1980:

A round, red Christmas ornament hanging in a window, sways and taps gently on the window if the house rocks north-south. An east-west jolt makes a small barometer swing against another window. None of the windows in the lodge has broken yet.

A clock in the lodge's main room will stop for a good-sized north-south jolt. The next north-south jolt will restart it, Truman said, but an east-west movement won't.

But what Harry really wanted to talk about that day were the letters he'd received from children all over the country responding to news that he refused to leave his home.

"Aren't these letters something?" he asked, waving a sheaf of them. "Those kids really care about me. And look how they indent paragraphs and how neat the letters are. Those kids are no dummies."

Some of the children's comments:

"If I lived on that mountain, I would be off right now."—Lisa Graham.

"Do the sane thing. One reason is because you should have a longer life. (Harry snorted at that. He'll be 84 on October 20.) Also you should save those poor cats and the dog you live with."—Carol Yee.

"Do you have a family? If you do, why not go back to them? I don't think you would enjoy being covered with steaming, boiling lava."—Kerry Roth.

"If the mountain erupted you would be burned and it would hurt."—Nick Chanich.

"You can replace a house or lodge or something like that but you can't replace YOU."—Elizabeth Goldner.

Greg and I waved at Harry on our way down the mountain later that day. He was shoveling the last of the snow off the walk in front of his lodge.

The mountain exploded 15 days later, at 8:32 A.M., May 18, a Sunday.

Climbers on Mounts Rainier, Adams, and Hood, within easy sight of Mount St. Helens, heard nothing. But along the Oregon coast 116 miles from the mountain, Mrs. Clara Fairfield heard a "house-shaking, window-rattling" boom. Her daughter in Portland, 45 miles from the mountain, heard nothing.

Luckily for us all, Mrs. Fairfield was a curator at the Oregon Museum of Science and Industry, and her curiosity led to a project to map the extent of the sound.

I wrote in the *Seattle Times* on December 7, 1980:

The results were surprising. The "quiet zone" around the mountain where the eruption was not heard or barely heard was much larger than expected.

The quiet zone was oval-shaped, extending about 200 miles north-south from Olympia to Albany, Oregon, and about 135 miles east-west from Oysterville and Manzanita, just north and south of the Columbia River's mouth, to The Dalles, Oregon.

But in Hamilton, Montana, 400 miles east of the volcano, the sound was described as resembling "very heavy artillery fire, very close by."

Persons in the San Juan Islands said later they wondered if Canadian gunboats were having gunnery practice.

Mary Lou, in our home in Shoreline, heard what sounded like a screen door slamming shut. As scoutmaster of Shoreline Troop 319, I was with the troop on a Camporee at Fort Lewis (now Joint Base Lewis-McChord or JBLM). I may have heard a moderate boom but, being at a military installation, thought nothing of it. It was an hour before I learned what had happened as the *Times* tried to find out where I was. A few hours later I was flying to Vancouver, awed at the massive cloud of ash still pouring from the mountain.

Harry Truman, perhaps still asleep in his lodge at 8:32 A.M., may not have heard anything. The bulging north side of the mountain collapsed and began sliding toward Spirit Lake. It covered Timberline at the end of the road. Luckily, no one was there.

Within seconds, it swept away and covered Harry's lodge. His body was never found. I think he would have preferred it that way. He really didn't want to leave the mountain.

❦   ❦   ❦

I was in the Mount St Helens crater with Mike Korosec, a geologist with the state Department of Natural Resources, in February of 1981, about eight months after that explosive eruption. A few days before our visit, the mountain had erupted again, more quietly, to double the size of a lava dome that now rose 450 feet above the floor of the crater. Korosec was there to take samples of the dome.

This was the mountain's third attempt at dome building to fill the crater. A dome that began rising soon after the May 1980 eruption was blown out by a July eruption. The next one began rising in August 1980, and was blown out two months later.

The dome I was looking at had begun building four months earlier and had doubled its size near Christmas and again the week before our visit.

Korosec told me that a series of lesser, but ash producing, eruptions had raised the floor of the crater hundreds of feet above where it had been after the big eruption.

"Material that has blown out and then fallen back has built up the floor," he said.

My story in the *Seattle Times* the next day:

The scene resembled a medieval painting of hell. Steam poured out of cracks running across the floor of the crater. Steam clouds sometimes blotted out the sun, barely peeking over the south rim of the gaping pit. Where steam pushed its way out from under a boulder, it hissed.

The smell of sulfur was everywhere. Here and there were boulders of a garish yellow, coated by sulfur fumes. I stooped to pick up a small rock with a bright yellow spot. Nice to take home for the kids. I yanked my hand back in surprise. The rock was more than hot enough to burn skin. I looked for a cooler rock.

Korosec, edging closer to the massive dome, suddenly seemed to be floating as steam obscured his legs.

A piece of the dome, perhaps dislodged by more lava pushing inside, broke off and made a small avalanche to the base. The slide was followed by furious steaming, the steam tinged yellow-brown this time.

"That's why you don't want to get too close to the dome," Korosec observed.

I stepped over a rock crevice about two feet wide. Steam was coming out. I was startled to feel heat radiating against my face. I went back and leaned over the crevice. Sure enough, it felt like sticking your face in a hot oven.

Except for the sulfur smell, it was almost pleasant in the crater, even with the ugly, cracked dome looming overhead. The crater walls shielded us from the wind.

The dome is as high as a 45-story building. But in that awesome setting—the yawning crater, the big blue sky to the north where part of the mountain has been blown away, and Mount Rainier looming in the distance—it didn't seem that high.

Hours later at my typewriter I could smell sulfur in my clothes and hair.

❦   ❦   ❦

Occasionally I've cried on company time. Usually it would be a story about sick or injured kids. This time was a few days after the catastrophic 1980 eruption of Mount St. Helens and I was back in the office writing for the Sunday paper.

The phone rang. It was Tom Johnston, father of David Johnston, the young geologist who had died in the eruption. I had been with Dave on the mountain's flanks a few days before the mountain blew. There were frequent earthquakes, small but near enough to rock a car on its springs. If I had known the quakes were caused by molten rock rising inside the mountain, I'd have been terrified.

Dave probably knew but calmly went about his work. I wrote about him then, and when he died I wrote again about his consuming interest in volcanoes, how he had dared to go in the hot crater to collect crucial samples, where he could feel the quakes though his boots, and how he had almost lost his life a few years earlier in a volcanic eruption in Alaska.

One of Dave's co-workers took my story with him when he flew back to Illinois to be with Dave's parents.

Tom Johnston's voice trembled as he thanked me for writing the story about his son, but he held himself together. So did I until I hung up. Then I turned to the wall and wept silently. My old friend, Stan Patty, the only one nearby, pretended not to notice.

At Sea in the Pacific Northwest

T HE COAL-FIRED STEAMSHIP *Umatilla* tore open its hull and jolted to a stop on uncharted rocks a few miles off the Washington coast on the night of February 8, 1884.

The captain, Frank Worth, and crewmen made it to shore where Makah Indians from the village of Ozette helped them through the surf. William Hanlon and another crewman stayed aboard the stricken ship, waiting for high tide to get off the rocks. Eventually the ship was freed, temporarily patched up and towed to a bay near Victoria where it sank. But it was raised, refitted and began an "afterlife" that I'll get to in a minute.

An interesting note is that President Chester A. Arthur asked Congress for "an appropriation for rewarding the services of the Makah Indians in rescuing and caring for the crew of the American steamer *Umatilla.*" I don't know if the Indians ever got the reward.

The rocks that did the damage have been known ever since as the Umatilla Reef, named for the ship that came to grief there. The dangerous reef was added to marine charts within a few years, but it wasn't until 1897 that a lightship, a ship that acts as a lighthouse, was stationed there. The lightship at Umatilla Reef, one of five along the West Coast, warned mariners of those rocks until September 30, 1971, when it was replaced by a buoy with an automated light and whistle. The ship's final signal: "Off station, all navigation aids secured."

During that last year I wanted to visit the ship and write a story about the vanishing lightships. I almost made it in

December of 1970. The Coast Guard agreed to take me and Roy Scully, a *Times* photographer, along on a mail run to the ship to talk to the crew and get a feel for the isolated life aboard. And I wanted to visit the lighthouse on Tatoosh Island, also scheduled to be automated. So the Coast Guard took Roy and me out to the lighthouse where we spent afternoon and night, planning to join the mail run the next morning. But the weather deteriorated overnight; the wind came up and it even snowed on Tatoosh. The mail run was canceled. Instead, we got a rough ride in a Coast Guard cutter back to Neah Bay. I never got aboard the lightship, and the automated light replaced it within a year.

With shipboard radar and GPS on modern ships, it's interesting to remember when the West Coast from Cape Mendocino to Vancouver Island was marked by lights— both lighthouses and lightships. Except for a few short dark stretches, the lights overlapped. The helmsman could see the next light ahead before the one astern faded from view.

Umatilla Reef's last lightship was built in 1946 on Lake Michigan. It was 128 feet long, powered by diesel engines. After duty off the Massachusetts coast, it passed through the Panama Canal to the West Coast and replaced an older ship at Umatilla Reef in 1961. It stayed at the reef until 1971.

It was isolated, hard duty for the crew, numbering about a dozen. The Coast Guard took over operation of lightships in 1940 from the Light House Service, and reduced tours of duty from four months to 30 days. Personnel considered lightship assignments almost equivalent to punishment. Umatilla Reef, exposed to winds from all directions, was considered the toughest duty of the five lightships along the West Coast.

In storms, the ship pitched and rolled so that crewmen sometimes had to hang on with both hands, making it difficult to carry out their work. In the worst storms, one crewman remembered, "the ones who weren't seasick were starving" because the galley couldn't operate. The most violent of the ship's contortions, the ones that knocked men out of their bunks, were when the chain to the four-ton mushroom anchor went taut and suddenly snubbed up the pitching ship.

When fog prevented good visibility for the light, the foghorn sounded every 30 seconds or so, vibrating through the ship, the kind of rumbling sound that makes your chest rattle. The ship at Umatilla Reef also had a submarine bell, operated by compressed air, extending 25 or 30 feet below the hull. The bell signal, which identified the ship, could be heard 10 to 15 miles away by ships with listening devices.

Lightships on the West Coast typically were painted red. Their station names were painted in six-foot-high white letters on the sides.

When the Coast Guard retired the Umatilla lightship, it gave the ship to a youth group in Seattle. It was in Seattle a few years until a stevedoring firm bought it to use as a bunkhouse for crews loading log ships in Ketchikan.

The *Swiftsure* lightship, the oldest still outfitted with its original steam engine—and one that in its early days used sails to help it keep on station—was retired in Seattle and for a few years moored at the park at the south end of Lake Union. It served as the San Francisco lightship and ended its active life as a relief

Swiftsure lightship. *Photo by Mike Boucher. Courtesy United States Lighthouse Society.*

lightship on stations at the Columbia River, Umatilla Reef and Swiftsure Bank off the entrance to the Strait of Juan de Fuca. Its colorful history includes being rammed by a steam schooner and in 1905 rescuing 155 passengers from a coastal steamer that had gone aground near Cape Mendocino.

So what about the "afterlife" of the *Umatilla*, the ship that ripped its hull open on the reef that still bears its name? The old iron steamship, after repairs on Vancouver Island, went into service in Japan for the Admiral Oriental Line. At some later point, the ship stranded off the coast of Japan. All 55 persons aboard were removed safely, but the old ship was considered a hopeless wreck and abandoned.

But a sand bar gradually built up between the wreck and the shore enabling salvagers to dismantle the ship, iron plate by iron plate. Obtaining the original plans from the American builder, they reassembled the vessel and it operated many more years as a Japanese steamship.

The light on Tatoosh Island was automated in 1977 and its last year-round inhabitants, a Coast Guard family, went to another assignment, leaving the island without permanent residents for the first time since the light lit up in 1857.

It is a flat-topped island, atop near-vertical 100-foot cliffs. The Coast Guard had a derrick that lifted supplies—and people—up from visiting boats. That was how Roy and I arrived in December of 1970. We stood on a flat, wooden pallet with only the lifting ropes to hang onto. The boat crew thought it was funny to start the pallet spinning as we lifted off the rolling boat. So Roy and I, hanging onto the ropes, spun dizzily as we were hoisted up 100 feet. At the top, we transferred to a small tractor and as it bumped along my overnight bag fell off and was run over by a wheel. It became a family joke—my bag being run over by a Coast Guard tractor—on Tatoosh Island.

The light is 165 feet above the sea—100 feet of cliff and 65 feet of tower—making it one of the highest lights on the coast.

The storms on Tatoosh can be epic. On February 11, 1911, the wind knocked down John M. Cowen, lighthouse keeper, and blew him 300 feet across the island top. Luckily he lodged in bushes. The same storm blew the family's bull off the island into the sea. The animal managed to swim ashore.

The Coast Guard cleaned up the island and removed most buildings in the 1990s. Workers restored a fence around a tiny cemetery with the graves of two children, a reminder of the lighthouse families who once called Tatoosh Island home.

⬦   ⬦   ⬦

The distress call came in just after dark on a stormy November night in 1971. Within minutes, a 52-foot Coast Guard boat, the *Intrepid*, left the lifeboat station in Coos Bay, Oregon, and headed for the bar where 20-foot waves were breaking. The fruitless search had gone on for an hour and a half when suddenly, at 8:57 P.M., the shore station lost contact with the *Intrepid*. It was 45 minutes before those on shore knew what had happened, or even that anyone was still alive.

A few days later I heard the amazing story of what had happened that night. The *Intrepid* with three men aboard had rolled all the way over—360 degrees. Now it's not too unusual for lifeboats to roll upside down—180 degrees—and then come back the same way they had gone over. But all the way around, with three men aboard?

I phoned the station in Coos Bay and talked to Daniel Sutherland, 29, the chief petty officer who was at the *Intrepid's* helm that night. He had 11 years in the Coast Guard, seven of them spent running lifeboats in the surf. I remember his quiet, unexcited way of telling me what had happened that night. This is what he told me:

Like the other crewmen, Sutherland was strapped to his station and was wearing a diver's wet suit and a crash helmet. They were about two miles out, Sutherland said, and he had just brought the boat through a 20-foot breaker with no problem.

"My engineer hollered 'look out' and I looked up and the curl of the breaker was already over the boat and falling. It was solid water, 30 to 35 feet high.

"It looked like the whole sky was falling on us. You could hear it starting to whistle then. Usually, working in them at night, you can hear the rumble once they break, and get ready for them. This one hadn't broken yet and it caught us unawares because there was no noise until it fell on us. It hit us before I could even hit the throttle.

"It hit us with a force I haven't felt before and I've been through a lot of breakers."

The breaker rolled the boat completely over, 360 degrees.

"And when we came up out of the first one, it took us another 180 degrees," Sutherland said. "I don't how long we were under water. You have no sense of time or direction when you're upside down in the water. All you know is that there's a tremendous force pulling at you from a lot of different directions at the same time. About all you remember is the force of the water and getting smashed into stuff and hearing your helmet bang into the mast and wheel and deck and whatever else it hits. I hung on to the wheel when we started over but the water peeled me off there like a wet rag."

The boat had barely recovered from its roll-and-a-half when it began speeding, bow first, down the front of a big wave.

"The boat was just plain surfing down the face of that wave," Sutherland said. "The bow would shear off in different directions with such force that it threw me to the deck, even hanging on. I climbed back on my feet three times and it would shear off in another direction and just wipe my feet out from under me."

When the wave finally let go of the boat, Sutherland discovered that a crew member, John C. Rehberg, 24, was missing. So was the strap that had held him to his station. The force of the water had ripped apart the weld holding the strap to the deck.

The third member of the crew, James R. Epperson, 27, still groggy from a blow on the head during the roll, spotted Rehberg waving a small light. Sutherland took the *Intrepid* alongside and he and Epperson helped Rehberg, still wearing his safety belt, back aboard.

"What we were scared of," Sutherland said, "was that there were another two or three waves in the series behind that big one. If more breakers of that size had hit us, we would have been hurting pretty bad. But the Good Lord couldn't help hearing us that night. We were yelling to him pretty loud."

Rehberg had been wearing Coast Guard-issue boots, laced up and tied. The water had taken them off, socks and all. It had peeled a tennis shoe off Sutherland's foot and zipped-up wet-suit boots from Epperson's feet. Rehberg and Epperson were both missing their crash helmets. Epperson found bits of crushed helmet in his hair.

"How the water took those helmets off without taking their heads along with them, I don't know," Sutherland said.

He paused, then said, "You can't even talk to a man about a breaker unless he's been in one. He'd think you were lying to him."

The Coast Guard Academy's *Alumni Association Bulletin* reprinted my story, commenting, "Our Pacific Northwest lifeboat men are a unique breed—perhaps the finest small-boat operators in the world along the nation's most rugged coastline."

The *Intrepid*, built in 1963, is still in Coast Guard service at Coos Bay, its outstanding record of service exceeded only by the men and women of the Coast Guard who save lives and property along the Oregon-Washington coastline.

❧   ❧   ❧

I was surprised as the submarine *Nautilus*, the world's first nuclear powered submarine, slipped beneath the surface of Puget Sound. I had been on submarines before and remembered the ear-popping change of pressure when they dived. There was none of that here.

A little earlier as I descended into the big submarine still at the pier, I had been impressed with the spaciousness of the interior, a stark contrast to the cramped compartments and passageways of submarines of that time.

The *Nautilus* visited Puget Sound in 1957. As a reporter for the *Seattle Times,* I was assigned to write about it.

The *Nautilus* was big: 320 feet long, a beam of 27 feet. And it was a big deal, the first of today's Navy fleet of nuclear-powered surface ships and submarines. During World War I, submarines were powered by batteries that periodically needed recharging by diesel engines. Diesel engines need air so submarines had to surface for recharging.

The Germans during World War II began building their U-boats with snorkels, air-breathing devices enabling them to run on diesel-engine power at periscope depth. The snorkel consisted of two pipes to the surface, one inhaling fresh air, the other releasing engine exhaust.

The *Nautilus*, the world's first nuclear submarine, in 1954. *Courtesy wireless-designmag.com*

By 1957 when the *Nautilus* visited Puget Sound, America's submarine fleet had mostly converted to snorkels which accounted for the pressure changes and noisy operation I remembered.

The *Nautilus* was quiet. And it was fast, a then-stunning 20 knots (23 m.p.h.) submerged. I don't know what speed we were running during the several hours we were submerged but I remember the sub banked into turns, like an airplane.

The *Nautilus* was powered by a pressurized-water reactor. The reactor fuel was enriched uranium, similar to the fuel in today's civilian power reactors. The reaction, uranium atoms knocked apart by neutrons, released energy mostly as heat.

Water under high pressure (to keep it from boiling) was piped past the reaction, heated to an extremely high temperature and then piped through another source of water that was heated to steam. The steam turned the turbine that generated electricity that ran the ship. The steam was condensed and used again, as was the pressurized water.

I walked back to look at the reactor. It appeared very ordinary to a nonscientist's eye, although I was awed to consider what was happening there.

The *Nautilus*'s first skipper, Capt. Eugene P. Wilkinson, a decorated veteran of submarine warfare in World War II, was still in command that day in 1957. The *Nautilus* had made its maiden voyage two years earlier and as it eased into Long Island Sound, he sent the message: "Underway on nuclear power," as brief as it was history-making.

It began a new era for submarines. They could cruise submerged at relatively high speed almost indefinitely. The propulsion system did not need air and needed refueling only after years of operation. A year after its visit to Puget Sound, the *Nautilus* steamed across the top of the world under the Arctic ice pack, stopping briefly at the North Pole.

The *Nautilus* was decommissioned in 1980 after steaming half a million miles in almost a quarter-century of service. It is at the Submarine Force Museum in Groton, Connecticut, near where it was built.

The Navy gave me a big photograph of the *Nautilus* on the surface laying down white water on a sharp turn. It was signed by Captain Wilkinson, Rear Admiral E.W. Grenfell, commander of submarine forces in the Pacific, and Senator Henry W. Jackson, all of whom were aboard that day. Senator Jackson died in 1983, Admiral Grenfell in 1980, and Captain Wilkinson in 2013.

I framed the photo and it hangs in our home near a painting of the *U.S.S. Constitution,* "Old Ironsides," that my father purchased many years ago and that hung in the home I grew up in. The ship is a wooden-hull, three-masted frigate launched in 1797 and is the oldest commissioned Navy vessel still afloat.

The *Nautilus* and "Old Ironsides" continue to share a room in our home.

On Land in the Pacific Northwest

T̲HE COLUMBIA RIVER'S PLACE in our lives was large. We swam in it, skated on it, drank from it, drove boats on it. It was a part of us and our country.

I first saw the fabled Cascades of the Columbia River from the passenger car of a railroad that runs along the north bank. I was young and about all I remember is tumbling white water, black rocks, and blowing spray...like old black-and-white snapshots.

That dangerous, spectacular stretch of river disappeared forever a few years later, covered by the pool behind Bonneville Dam. The Cascades had been a real obstacle to river traffic. Steamboats could not go upriver through the rapids and could go downstream only at great risk—although a few made it.

William Clark of the Lewis and Clark Corps of Discovery got a good long look at the Cascades in 1805. By that time he had seen a lot of country, a lot of rivers, but his journal entries still reflected awe:

"This Great Chute or falls is about ½ mile with the water of this great river compressed within the space of 150 paces in which there is great numbers of both large and small rocks, water passing with great velocity foaming and boiling in a most horrible manner, with a fall of about 20 feet."

The Lewis and Clark party portaged around the falls, carrying their baggage and lowering empty canoes by ropes held from the shore. And Clark's description was only of the upper half of the Cascades. The river fell 40 feet over several miles.

An Indian legend about the Cascades told that at one time it had been possible to walk across the river on a natural bridge. White people gave the term "Bridge of the Gods" to the area, a name that persists today on a highway bridge spanning the river above Clark's Great Chute.

As it turned out, the Indians knew what they were talking about.

I wrote in the *Seattle Times* in 1978 that the Indians told the first white arrivals that the Cascades of the Columbia River had not always been there. "Time was, they said, when canoes could travel from sea level to Celilo Falls near The Dalles without obstruction. But, the Indian story went, the river once was dammed up at that place, causing a huge lake to form upstream. As the river cut its way through the obstruction, the Cascades appeared. Modern geological investigation has pretty much confirmed the Indian story of what happened."

A massive landslide from what is now the north or Washington State side of the river, perhaps triggered by an earthquake, closed the river canyon and even slid a little way up the Oregon side. The natural dam would have been two or three hundred feet above the old river bed.

When the river eventually cut through the natural dam and left the narrow, tumbling, rock-filled channel, the stream had been pushed a mile and a half toward the Oregon side. That bend is still in the river.

No one knows how long it took the river to cut through the dam, but until it did it might have been possible to walk from one side to the other.

When did the mountainside on the north side of the river slide and form the dam? Dates based on radiocarbon tests on trees drowned in the lake behind the dam cluster around 700 or 800 years ago, although there are more recent estimates.

Some believe the Cascades of the Columbia gave its name to the Cascade Range of mountains it penetrates. The Pacific Crest Trail crosses the Columbia River on today's steel-and-concrete Bridge of the Gods. It is the lowest point on the 2,650-mile trail between the Mexican and Canadian borders.

The Cascades of the Columbia, a violent, colorful part of our past, lives on in my memory—like old black-and-white snapshots.

❧   ❧   ❧

My family visited Celilo Falls, the ancient fishing place for Indians on the Columbia River, when my sisters and I were young and living in Pasco, probably in the mid-1930s. I remember Dad bought a salmon from an Indian fisherman. It was a good sized fish, probably ten pounds or so. The price: 25 cents.

Dad probably told us we were visiting a place famous in history, dreaded by steamship captains because the narrow, rocky channels with drops of as much as 20 feet blocked navigation, but valued by the Indians who had fished there for thousands of years.

I returned to Celilo Falls in the fall of 1956, another fishing season for the Indians—and the last forever at Celilo. The turbulent place where the river, usually a mile or more across, squeezed into a channel not much more than 140 feet wide, would soon disappear. The Dalles Dam, nearing completion eight or nine miles downstream, would close the channel in a few months and the rising pool behind it would cover and silence the falls, ending the roar that had always been there, the roar that was part of the place.

Celilo Falls, 1956. *Author photo.*

It was warm that fall day in 1956 as I approached the rocky channel. Spray drifting from the falls felt good. Men with long-handled dip nets stood on rickety-looking platforms built over the churning water. Most had lifelines, sturdy ropes around their waists linked to something solid on the shore. I guess the rope would save lives, I thought, but falling into churning water, swept away until the rope snubbed you up, being hauled back half drowned, scraping and bumping against rock wouldn't be much fun.

On a good day you could see the salmon struggling to climb the falls, the whole body working frantically as the fish, hanging almost vertically, advanced, held...and then fell back to the quieter pool below the falls to recover for another effort. The fishermen swept their nets through the pools to capture a resting salmon, and hoisted the wildly flopping fish up to the platform, conked it on the head with a rock or pipe to end the flopping, and passed it ashore.

Most of the migrating salmon did make it over Celilo Falls, maintaining for thousands of years the salmon runs far upstream in the Columbia and Snake Rivers and their many tributaries.

There is archeological evidence that Indians had fished at Celilo for at least 10,000 years and that it was a major trading center during fishing season. Tribes from the American Southwest, the Great Plains and the California and British Columbia coasts traded their goods for dried salmon.

The westbound Lewis and Clark party reached Celilo in late October 1805. They descended by a combination of portaging some of their most valuable items around the worst falls and using the party's best swimmers to get the lightened canoes through. Though it was a little past peak fishing time, still Clark counted 107 stacks of dried, pounded salmon that he estimated must have contained 10,000 pounds of fish.

There were not many fish on the day I visited in the fall of 1956. The men on the platforms were waiting, holding their nets, watching the pools below the falls.

I wanted to get photographs so I climbed into sort of a box suspended from a cable running to a rocky island and began pulling myself across a channel to where several men were fishing. I felt tugs on the rope as a young guy on the island helped pull me across. I thanked him and he said: "I'm going back. You can pull me if you like."

I talked to one of the fisherman: "Not many fish today," I began. "Nope, pretty quiet," one responded.

I wondered if they were thinking about the fact that the falls would soon be drowned, that the salmon would have free passage upstream, that the traditional fishery at this place would be history. "The last year, I guess," I offered. A stoic reply: "Yep, the last time."

Regretfully we said goodbye to that spectacular, thundering river channel. These fishermen must have been thinking of their ancestral fishing place that would soon be drowned. But I guess there wasn't much they could say. Words wouldn't dismantle the dam the Army Corps of Engineers was building downstream.

The Army closed the steel and concrete gates of The Dalles Dam the morning of March 10, 1957, a few months after my last visit, and the pool began to rise. Several hundred people at Celilo Falls were watching as, about six hours later, the rising reservoir covered the falls and silenced the ancient roar. Silenced it forever. I'm just as glad I wasn't there.

But a half century later, even the Army Corps of Engineers must have been a little sentimental about Celilo Falls. In 2008, the agency used sonar to probe the old channel at Celilo. The study found the submerged falls were not yet blanketed by silt collecting behind the dam. The study reported the "rocky outcrops, carved basins and channels" matched photographs from the 1940s.

❧   ❧   ❧

Homely Rapids, now buried in the pool behind McNary Dam on the Columbia River near Umatilla, Oregon, was still exposed on a summer Sunday, probably in 1950, when a friend and I took a boat through. (The rapids were pronounced HAHM-lee, sometimes spelled Homley.)

As it turned out, it was a relaxing outing. The rapids looked formidable as we approached from upstream—protruding rocks, white water, swift currents. But my friend, Joe Van

Vliet, turned his outboard boat around and backed through the rapids. He could control how fast we descended and pick the best channels. We didn't touch a rock. Returning later in the day, heading forward this time, Joe again carefully picked the best way through.

Out of curiosity I looked in the journals of Lewis and Clark to see what they thought of Homely Rapids as they descended them on the afternoon of October 18, 1805. Clark noted they landed for a few minutes to inspect the rapids before going through them. He described them as "verry bad."

The river would have been lower in October, making the passage more difficult to navigate through rapids in their heavily loaded dugout canoes than in our small outboard boat.

Joe and I went on down the river a few miles beyond the rapids, past the mouth of the Walla Walla River, and into Wallula Gap where the Columbia cuts a spectacular channel through cliffs, layers of volcanic rock that poured over the land millions of years ago. Clark described the Gap as where "the river passes into the range of the high country...high clifts...200 feet above the water...black, rugid rocks."

A bit downstream from the Gap, Clark noted a distant mountain "bearing SW, a conical form covered with snow." That would be Mount Hood, named almost exactly thirteen years before Clark saw it by Lieutenant William Broughton of Captain George Vancouver's crew.

A year or so after our trip through Homely Rapids, I was writing stories for the *Tri-City Herald* about the construction of McNary Dam downstream from Wallula Gap. Workers had built cofferdams that exposed the bedrock channels of the river, the site of Umatilla Rapids, more extensive and potentially dangerous to river traffic than Homely Rapids.

Hill Williams Jr. and another reporter at the site of the McNary Dam construction. *Author photo.*

Early-day steamboats could pass Umatilla Rapids during times of high water. But they were a barrier during low water, cutting off river navigation upstream in the Columbia and Snake Rivers.

I went down inside the cofferdams and took photographs of the exposed river bed carved by thousands of years of rushing water, wondering if the rocks I was standing on had ever torn the bottom out of a steamboat.

The reservoir behind McNary Dam began rising in 1954, covering not only Umatilla Rapids but Homely Rapids that Joe and I had navigated.

❧   ❧   ❧

I wrote about the Columbia River many times. It dumps the most water—and the most sediment from an eroding continent—into the Pacific Ocean of any river in the Western Hemisphere. From the Bering Sea to the tip of South America, it is unequaled.

The mighty river I remember has been tamed. Its flow has been slowed by fourteen dams, three in British Columbia and eleven in the river's path through and around Washington State.

The mightiest of those dams, fitting for a mighty river, is Grand Coulee Dam, one mile long, 550 feet high, backing its lake 151 miles to the Canadian border. It is the heaviest concrete structure ever built, a gravity dam. The river, mighty as it is, will never push the dam out of its channel.

The dam's first generator began producing electricity in January 1941, several years before nuclear work at Hanford became a big customer. Today the dam generates electrical power that is supplied to eleven western states and Canada.

Huge canals scooped out after World War II began carrying irrigation water from the dam's reservoir to the arid Columbia Basin, today one of the world's major food-producing areas.

The dams slowed the Columbia's currents and covered its rapids. But it is still the mighty river of the West. Its flow dilutes ocean water as far as 300 miles off its mouth. Its drainage basin includes much of Washington, Oregon, Idaho, and Montana, slivers of Nevada, Utah, and Wyoming and big chunks of British Columbia and Alberta.

The Columbia is old, very old. Its existence can be documented with a fair amount of confidence to 15 million years. It is probably much older.

Geologists know the river was in place before the Cascade Range began rising 10 to 15 million years ago because the river cuts through the range. If the mountains had been there first, the river would have found another way.

Instead, the river dug away persistently as the mountains began trying to block its channel. Sometimes the river fell behind the rising barrier and a great lake formed east of the Cascades. At other times, perhaps when the rate of mountain building slowed or the river flow increased, the river regained lost ground, cut a deeper channel and the lake drained.

The Columbia may be as old as 100 million years, dating back to the birth of the Rocky Mountains. If the river was there then, it would have flowed more or less straight west from the Rockies to the Pacific, right over the yet-unborn Cascades. But no one really knows beyond about 15 million years.

The river achieved a dubious distinction in the 1940s, '50s and '60s as the most radioactive river in the free world, perhaps the whole world.

The original plutonium-producing reactors at Hanford used "once-through" cooling systems. River water was pumped through the operating reactor just once and then sent to open-air ponds for several days of cooling, both thermally and radioactively, before returning to the river.

When all eight once-through reactors were operating at Hanford, several thousand curies of radioactivity a day went into the river (a curie is a measure of radioactivity). With today's standards, a spill of one curie would attract attention.

Radioactive material from Hanford once could be found in marine life all along the Washington coast and even into Puget Sound. Traces of radioactive zinc from Hanford were found in tuna off San Diego in 1970. But despite intensive studies, no evidence of harm to the river, marine animals, or plants was ever found.

The last Hanford reactor with once-through cooling closed down in 1971.

There is still enough radioactive debris in the river's sediments to interest researchers, but they have to dig to find it. The top layers—the youngest—no longer contain any radioactive material bearing Hanford's fingerprint. Deeper layers reflect the story of Hanford's work during World War II and the Cold War, a record a little like those contained in tree rings.

But the upper layers do hold plutonium from China's nuclear tests.

❧   ❧   ❧

The years after the end of World War II were exciting times in the Columbia Basin. Dreams by generations of homesteaders, politicians, business owners and newspaper editors of irrigating dry land were about to come true. Construction of Grand Coulee Dam, built during the Depression, had begun producing electrical power in 1941. Another purpose, irrigating 600,000 acres with Columbia River water, was delayed during the war. But now big canals to carry water were being scooped out.

But, oddly, the first water to reach thirsty land didn't come from anywhere near the new Grand Coulee Dam that made the project possible, or giant pumps that today lift water from behind the dam to the network of canals that carry it across the Columbia Basin. Rather, the first water pumped from the river flowed a hundred miles downstream from Grand Coulee, lifted to what they called Block 1, about 5,400 acres along the river just upstream from Pasco.

A little before noon on May 15, 1948, the first irrigation water from the vast Columbia Basin Irrigation Project flowed onto sagebrush-spotted land destined for farms.

Block 1 comprised a tiny fraction of the acreage that would eventually be watered by the project. But it was a big deal for the eastern Washington businessmen and politicians who had been working for the dam and irrigation for more than 40 years.

I was there that day. I wished my grandfather, who had homesteaded 160 dry acres of Columbia Basin near the turn of the century, could have seen it. The climate had favored William L. Williams with unusually wet years at the beginning of the 1900s as he built a home, cleared sagebrush, and planted crops to earn ownership of the land near Quincy. Wheat grew fairly well even though the land was not really suitable for dry-land wheat farming. But within a decade or so, the rain and snow decreased and crop yields weren't paying expenses. My grandfather sold the farm and the family moved to Pullman where my father, in high school, would be able to afford college. My grandfather's original 160-acre homestead is under irrigation today.

Schemes of how the Columbia Basin could be watered dated back to the early 1900s. One of the more interesting ideas that never got beyond the talking stage was to dam the Pend Oreille River near Newport in the northeast corner of Washington State and convey water something like 130 miles through a system of canals, tunnels and reservoirs.

The dry years continued in the 1920s and '30s, increasing business and political pressure to irrigate the Columbia Basin. And, finally, construction of Grand Coulee Dam as a combined irrigation and hydroelectric power project began in 1934.

Although the dam was largely completed in 1941, it would be several years before the main canals could be built. Critics in Congress who had opposed the dam construction in the first place were threatening to cut funds for construction necessary for irrigation.

At least partly in an attempt to satisfy the critics, the Bureau of Reclamation selected Block 1 as sort of a demonstration to show what sagebrush land could produce with water. The bureau paid for a small system of canals and for a pumping plant on the river.

There probably were 200 or so people from all over the Columbia Basin at Block 1 to hear Franklin County Superior Court Judge B.B. Horrigan, a pioneer in the fight for irrigation, recall failed attempts in the past. He pointed to small abandoned ditches within sight of the ceremony, relics of earlier efforts. Then, at his signal, a wave of the hand relayed by Boy Scouts, the pump a quarter mile away started up and water began flowing.

The government had offered farm units in Block 1 for sale to applicants who had at least some farming experience, were physically and mentally fit, had good character references and a net worth of at least $3,700. Veterans were given preference. There was so much interest that the government held more than 30 drawings. The first water that day went to land owned by O. C. Gillum, a winner in one of the drawings. He and his two young sons were there when the first water reached their land. One of the boys, Billy, stood in a ditch as water washed over his feet.

By the early 1950s big canals were reaching across the basin. Today Pasco Block 1 gets water from the Potholes Canal.

❦   ❦   ❦

Viewed from the wet side of Washington State, it may be surprising to learn that we have living, moving sand dunes in the dry side east of the Cascade Range.

Some of the most spectacular dunes are in an odd patch of land surrounded by farms about 15 miles north of Pasco.

Some are as high as 120 feet, sharply chiseled by wind. In a stiff breeze, however, the edges of the dunes dissolve into a blur as sand blows along, as it has for centuries.

But grasses have appeared on some of the dunes, the beginning of the end.

"The source of sand for the dunes has not yet been completely cut off," a geologist told me years ago. "But their major growth has stopped. Many are being vegetated, which stops their movement."

The dunes apparently originated 4,000 to 6,000 years ago when the Pacific Northwest experienced a warm, dry period. This allowed wind to stir up sediments from an ancient lake bottom formed by great floods near the end of the most recent ice age.

I wrote in the 1980s about a grove of juniper trees among those sand dunes, the northernmost appearance of juniper trees in North America. Their ages pose a minor mystery.

The Bureau of Land Management, which controls the land with the dunes and the junipers, told me there did not seem to be any young junipers in the grove. Test borings revealed the ages of the trees fell into three groups: about 160 years, 100 years, and 70 years (ages at the time of testing.)

"The only years you get seedling survival for these trees are the unusual summers that are wet and cool," a Bureau scientist told me. "That's why you see only a few age classes of trees out there."

The Bureau didn't go further but the junipers' ages bring up an interesting question about the origin of the trees: Is it possible the trees owe their existence to three of the greatest volcanic eruptions ever to occur in the world?

Tambora, an Indonesian volcano, erupted in 1815, described as the world's greatest recorded volcanic event. Krakatoa, also in Indonesia, erupted catastrophically in 1883. Both were remembered to have affected the climate.

And Katmai in Alaska erupted violently in June 1912, sending enough ash and dust into the upper atmosphere to rob the earth of 20 percent of the sun's heat that summer. I remember talking to old-timers who remembered 1912 as "the year without a summer."

Years since those eruptions, reported in the early 1980s when I talked to the scientists, fell pretty well into the junipers age classes.

The coincidence doesn't prove anything, of course. But the rough match between juniper-tree ages and volcanic eruptions is interesting.

Hanford High School. *Photo by Chad Erland. Courtesy, Hanford History Project, WSU Tri-Cities.*

❧   ❧   ❧

When the wind dropped I could hear my heart beating, not something you experience often in our noisy world. And the call of a meadowlark at least a quarter mile away.

The wind was moaning through the stone skeleton of the old Hanford School. The windows were gone in the two-story relic. You could see through it.

It was spring of 1981 and Roy Scully, a *Seattle Times* photographer, and I were wandering (with escort) the mostly silent Hanford Reservation, once part of the Manhattan Project to develop the atomic bomb. It had been almost 40 years since children's voices filled that old building, since a bell rang the end of classes and the doors burst open with kids on their way home.

This barren plateau lying above the Columbia River was not silent for long after those kids, their parents, and teachers had been moved out to make way for the Hanford atomic works. Heavy construction began almost immediately to build the world's first factory to create plutonium—ammunition for nuclear bombs.

Tens of thousands of workers recruited from all over America built the reactors, then thousands of technicians and scientists ran things through the end of World War II and into the Cold War. Then, one by one, the reactors went cold as the nation began reducing its nuclear arms.

Only one reactor was still operating the day Roy and I visited the silent reservation. It was out of sight upstream from us—the dual-purpose N Reactor that generated electrical power for the Pacific Northwest as well as producing plutonium. It shut down in 1987 after operating for 24 years.

As Roy shot pictures, I wondered about those pupils—middle-age by then—from both Hanford and White Bluffs who had attended that school. Where did they end up? Have they been back? Did they take advantage of government-sponsored tours to visit their former homes that had been reduced to foundations, or maybe just a fireplace built of stones taken from the nearby river? Did they rummage through debris looking for keepsakes?

Did they visit the skeleton of the old school? Did they notice that the trees in front of the school had died after they quit watering them decades ago?

It wasn't the only time that day I thought about the former residents of Hanford and White Bluffs.

Roy and I had checked out the former First Bank of White Bluffs, a small, square stone building that had been left standing for some reason. It was strangely alone, windowless and empty. The door of the vault still hung on its hinges but was unlocked as it had been since that last day.

And quite often we'd realize that a mule deer was staring at us from close range. They were bold at Hanford that day. No one had shot at them for more than 30 years.

❧   ❧   ❧

President Carter designated 1980 as the Year of the Coast in an effort to inform the public of the value of the nation's coastlines. I wrote this for the *Seattle Times* that year:

> Two harbor seals watched us as we waited, tired and frustrated, for the tide to allow us around a rocky headland that juts into the Pacific Ocean about 12 miles north of LaPush.
>
> My son, Tom, and I were nearing the end of the second day of a hike along this Washington wilderness coastline, about 45 miles of sandy beaches, rocky cliffs, tumbled boulders and breathtaking scenery. We had started the morning before at Shi Shi Beach at the north end of the new part of the Olympic National Park's wilderness strip. We had made good time but here we were in late afternoon, stopped by the tide, out of drinking water and with no good place to camp.
>
> We were not in danger, but it promised to be a dry, uncomfortable night among rocks and driftwood. And there didn't seem to be any reasonable way over the headland.
>
> As I stared back into the seals' dark eyes, I reflected on the difficulty of adjusting to the rhythms of nature.
>
> Forgetting schedules and deadlines while on the beach had seemed an attractive idea while planning at home. Be one with nature. Go when the tide said go. Stop when the tide said stop.
>
> But the real thing turned out to be irritating. Tom, 14, adjusted better than I did. He settled down on a log with a paperback while I tried again to see if I could see around the point (I couldn't) or walked out again on the point to check the tide's level.

Always the two seals kept pace just off the beach, watching me carefully.

We were stuck and it bothered me. It wasn't so much the delay or even the prospect of an uncomfortable night. Rather, it was the realization that it is difficult, perhaps impossible, to shed the habits of a lifetime and adopt nature's pace.

It was late that mid-July evening before the tide receded enough for us to boulder-hop around the point.

Thirty minutes earlier I had felt like an irritable misfit in nature's plan. But now nature provided. We found a reasonably flat place of sandy beach for a camp, a big, flat log to put our stove on and a tiny stream cascading down rocks a few steps away.

The seals had disappeared as we ate a hot meal in pitch dark and then crawled into our sleeping bags.

Tom left the hike at LaPush, after three days and about 30 miles, to return to his job. After another 10 miles the next day, I was settling down for my last night out. Mary Lou would be waiting for me at the Hoh River trailhead the next afternoon.

In the dusk, the beach looked as it must have for hundreds or thousands of years. The only sign of civilization was a winking from the lighthouse on Destruction Island to the south. The light seemed companionable.

I felt good as I settled down. For once, I even felt as if nature and I were together instead of struggling.

But there's a goofy story about me and that campsite. A psychiatrist might have fun with it.

Late that afternoon I had walked past that good campsite, thinking I would add a few more miles to the day. But after a mile or so, I changed my mind and turned back.

I was puzzled over my surprising emotions as I returned to "my" campsite. I was tired and yet I had to consciously restrain myself from running to claim "my" spot.

I hadn't seen anyone for hours. I was sure I was the only hiker on that stretch of beach. Yet I wanted to run to claim my campsite.

A race to beat non-existent competitors to a good camping spot? Even the idea of "first come, first served" on such a lovely, spacious beach struck me as offensive.

I wondered as I drifted to sleep how long it would take to shed the pushiness of city life.

❧   ❧   ❧

Hikers on the trail from Lake Ozette to the ocean beach on the west edge of the Olympic Peninsula in the 1970s occasionally would meet Bill Lester, a friendly Olympic National Park ranger, pushing a wheelbarrow with a tarp draped over the cargo. Most assumed the load was tools or camp gear, or something.

But sometimes the tarp would heave and a black paw would slide out. Lester would stop, whip out a needle, give a groggy bear another "hit" and continue on his way.

Lester, or Ranger Bill as students at the nearby Washington State University archeological site called him, spent much of his time trying to solve "bear problems." Most were at the popular Sand Point campground, a beautiful forested spit jutting into the Pacific Ocean about three miles down the trail from Lake Ozette.

Campers who failed to maintain a clean camp and hang food out of reach of bears were the problem. But it was the bears that Ranger Bill would tranquilize, load in the wheelbarrow and trundle up to the ranger station. Once there, the bear would be loaded in a pickup and released far back in the hills.

❧   ❧   ❧

This is how I led a story in the *Seattle Times* on November 23, 1984—undoubtedly the most puzzling story I've ever written:

> Somehow, in a way that baffles geologists, a massive chunk of earth has been plucked from a remote plateau in North Central Washington and put down, right side up, 73 feet away.
>
> There is no evidence that humans had anything to do with it. Neither are there marks of machinery. The piece of earth, which remained largely intact during its move, is estimated to weigh at least three tons.
>
> "All we know for sure is this puzzle piece of earth is 73 feet away from the hole it came out of," said Greg W. Behrens, a geologist with the Bureau of Reclamation at Grand Coulee Dam.
>
> The displaced chunk is an irregular pear shape, 10 feet long and 7 feet wide. Its thickness varies from two feet at one end to about 18 inches at the other.
>
> The shape and thickness of the puzzle piece exactly match the hole that was left behind…The chunk was rotated counterclockwise about 20 degrees in comparison to the orientation of the hole it left behind.

On a dark November afternoon Behrens took Pete Liddell, *Times* photographer, and me cross-country in a four-wheel drive vehicle to view the displaced chunk and hole it came out of.

The puzzle piece had been discovered on October 18, about a month before Pete and I saw it, by two brothers on horseback rounding up cows. They believed the event occurred sometime after mid-September when they were last there harvesting wheat.

My story continued:

> Adding a bit of intrigue is the fact that there was a small earthquake in the area during that month-long period, at

8:24 P.M. October 9. The quake, measured at 3.0 on the Richter scale, was felt in towns in the area, but not at the nearest farmhouse a few miles from the mystery site.

The University of Washington pinpointed the quake's epicenter about 20 miles southwest of the displaced earth, and about four miles deep.

Don Auburton, director of mining for the Colville Tribe, told me: "There had been quite a roar with the earthquake so we wondered if perhaps a meteorite fragment had impacted and ripped out a piece of earth."

But geologists who viewed the site ruled out the meteorite possibility.

"There was no sign of impact," Auburton said. "The hole was not a crater. It had vertical walls and a fairly flat bottom. It was almost as though it had been cut out with a giant cookie cutter."

But, Auburton pointed out, even a giant cookie cutter could not have left the hole the way it was first found. Roots that had led to vegetation in the puzzle piece dangled from the vertical walls of the hole, indicating they had been torn apart rather than cut.

Behrens wondered if the earthquake's seismic waves in the bedrock had triggered concentric surface waves in the soil. If the waves converged, they might have ejected a piece of earth where they focused, he mused.

A University of Washington geophysicist agreed that focusing can occur but could not explain the tremendous energy required to pluck out a piece of earth weighing tons and move it 73 feet.

Although there was no sign that the chunk had been dragged or rolled the 73 feet, geologists found pieces on the ground that had dribbled from the chunk as it moved. Surprisingly, the dribbles traced an arc from divot to chunk although that could be explained by a stiff wind distributing the "dribblings" in a curve as the chunk rose and fell.

Almost 30 years after the puzzling event, I talked to Behrens, now retired. He still thought the idea of focused seismic waves provided the best possible explanation.

I ended that 1984 *Times* story with a quote from Lindsay McClelland of the Smithsonian Scientific Event Alert Network who said he was not aware of previous reports of similar occurrences. But he was interested in this one.

"Be sure to let me know if you find out what caused it," he told me.

I've never called him back.

◆　　◆　　◆

It seems unlikely. The summer sun has set and the glaciers and snowfields high on Mount Rainier are dark. Self-respecting animals should be asleep. But the activity is just beginning.

In one of nature's more surprising schemes the table has been set for dinner. And the guests—some of the creatures that make a living in the high-altitude ice—are going into action.

All through the day winds from the lush forests and meadows far below have been carrying tiny insects up the slopes of the mountain. As the winds drop, the load of insects is dumped on the snow and glacial ice.

John Edwards, then at the University of Washington, was one of the world's few specialists in alpine insects. He estimated that, at any one time, about 12 tons of insects are on the mountain above the 8,000-foot level.

"All day long, there is a steady rain of insects," he told me. "If you look closely, the snow is just littered with them. And when they land on the snow, they get cold and can't generate the energy to fly away."

Birds know about the insect bonanza and as long as there is light, they hop across the snow, feasting.

"The food is laid out on a white tablecloth," Edwards said, "and is not able to move."

❧   ❧   ❧

I probably talked too much when our family traveled. But it's a sly way to acquaint the children, a captive audience in the back seat, with the fascinating country we live in.

You don't have to travel far to find educational opportunities. By studying the south face of Mount Si, the side facing I-90 above North Bend, you can see how high the last ice sheets reached during the most recent ice age thousands of years ago, an elevation of about two thousand feet. Below that, Si is smooth. Above, the peak is still craggy.

And that can lead to conversation about the ice ages, and how ice carved the Cascades into the spectacular peaks we know today.

There are places in road cuts where you can see the thin, white streak laid down by some long-ago volcanic eruption. It's OK if you don't know the date of the eruption or even which volcano. The interesting thing is how geologists, who do know the date and mountain, use the ash layer to date other events in the earth's story. Rock below the ash layer is older; above is younger.

Perhaps the best-known ash layer of all is the one laid down over much of the Pacific Northwest when Mount Mazama in southern Oregon blew itself apart in a series of explosions about six thousand years ago.

What was left of the mountain collapsed, forming today's beautiful Crater Lake.

The smaller, more recent ash layer blasted out of Mount St. Helens in 1980 has become another dating layer for scientists.

Another lecture for your backseat audience: Heading east on the bridge across the Columbia River at Vantage you are facing a massive relic of one of the greatest outpourings of lava anywhere, anytime. Flows of the Columbia River Basalt issued repeatedly from great fissures in the earth, beginning about 15 million years ago.

Again and again over millions of years there were outpourings of lava, sometimes separated by thousands or a million years. As you cross the bridge at Vantage you are in the channel the Columbia has carved through some of those layers.

An unsuccessful exploratory effort to find oil and natural gas in another part of the Columbia Basin drilled through 10,000 feet of the basalt—and was still in basalt. Think of it: more than 10,000 feet of rock.

Family landmarks are another gimmick to interest your audience. I remember my father's story about working in the wheat harvest in eastern Washington and wearing a pair of socks so long that when he took them off the last time he hung them in a barn and never touched them again. With harvest ended, he went home to Pullman and left the socks hanging in the barn.

In later years when we drove the highway between Dusty and Colfax, he would point out the barn where we all assumed the socks were still hanging.

The story got us thinking and talking about wheat harvesting in the old days: the big teams of horses, the hot, grueling labor of filling and heaving sacks of wheat, compared to air-conditioned combines and wheat-hauling trucks on modern farms.

❧   ❧   ❧

It was swelteringly hot as we stopped at a viewing point for Grand Coulee Dam on our way home from Spokane. The atmosphere in the car was somewhat strained. The children were impatient to get home. The dog was panting pathetically in the back of the station wagon.

But Mary Lou and I considered a stop at the dam an "educational experience," an important part of growing up in the Pacific Northwest. We remembered when families would make annual trips to watch construction of the dam "one of the modern wonders of the world."

Despite their initial lack of enthusiasm for the stop, the children were impressed. No, that's not strong enough. They were overwhelmed. Water was spilling, sending cooling mist drifting to where we stood. The dam looked as big as the pyramids of Egypt.

Actually, the dam is bigger than the biggest pyramid in Egypt. It's always satisfying for parents when today lives up to our memories.

Even the dog was happy. It wisely sought the shade and breeze under our parked car.

❧   ❧   ❧

It was dark. Really dark. I couldn't see the settings on my camera. And I began to understand the fear of primitive people when they saw what I was witnessing—a total eclipse of the sun. Think about it: The dependable old sun that moves across the sky every day, unexpectedly turning off. The birds would have gone silent, as if the world was shutting down. It must have been terrifying.

But this was February 26, 1979, and the media had been full of news about the coming eclipse that would be total in a strip a hundred or so miles wide across eastern Washington, but only partial in Seattle. I was at Bickleton, a wheat-farming community of about 90 persons on the high rolling plateau between the Columbia and Yakima River Valleys. We were waiting there for the moon's shadow to pass over us as it crossed in front of the sun.

There were thin clouds the night before and picking an observation spot was tricky. We listened to early-morning radio reports and the forecasters said there was a belt of clear weather off the coast. Whether it would arrive over eastern Washington in time for the eclipse was iffy.

Bickleton, high in the Horse Heaven Hills, seemed about the best bet. We joined about 50 hopeful eclipse viewers in the lee of the Bickleton School District shop building, huddled together to stay out of a biting wind. Bickleton students had been joined by students and staff from the University of Puget Sound in Tacoma. Mary Lou and I had taken our kids out of school for the day. The educational value of viewing a total eclipse of the sun seemed more important than a day in classes.

We had passed people camped along the road, many with telescopes and cameras. They all looked cold as they stood beside old drifts of snow. We saw license plates from California, Oregon, Idaho, British Columbia.

A few minutes after 8 A.M., the scudding clouds thinned enough for us to see the sun as a dim ball of light with a bite already covered by the moon.

And then, as the moon almost covered the sun, the clouds drifted away enough that we saw "Bailey's Beads," the last glimpses of sunlight shining through the canyons of the moon.

As the sun went out, a cheer went up from the students. Just then the lights on the shop building went on. Everyone yelled, "Turn them off!" But they were controlled automatically and stayed on.

Venus and stars were visible during totality. The landscape had a dark, sickly pallor. Off to the south, across the Columbia River, the horizon was a bright, yellowish orange, apparently due to the sun shining beyond the moon's shadow.

As the moon moved across the sun, a few sparkles appeared on the trailing side of the moon, "Bailey's Beads" again as the sun peeked out. Then, as the moon slid further, the sparkles increased in intensity until it looked as if that side of the moon had caught fire. Finally, as the moon continued to move, a thin crescent of the sun emerged and began to grow.

I phoned a story to the *Times*, using a Bickleton School District telephone, the dependable means of communication in those pre-computer days.

An hour later the sky was blue and the sun was out. And a million years ago, our forefathers—and mothers—would have sighed with relief as their familiar world returned.

❧   ❧   ❧

Would you believe a museum 25 feet wide and 1,000 feet long? That would be the museum at Rocky Reach Dam on the Columbia River seven miles north of Wenatchee along Highway 97.

The dam's powerhouse was designed with the usual long, narrow concrete gallery for cables, switching gear and equipment storage. But the builder, the Chelan County Public Utility District, thought it could better use the gallery for a museum and talked designers into recessing cables and other equipment to leave the space free.

As good museums should, the Gallery of the Columbia at Rocky Reach reflects the country it springs from, particularly the river itself which has always bound the Big Bend country together.

A display that educated me: Getting wheat to market before railroads arrived was a problem for farmers and provoked some ingenious solutions.

One method was the "wheat pipe" built in 1896 by James E. Keane near Rock Island on the Columbia downstream from Wenatchee. It consisted of 2,600 feet of 6-inch, galvanized pipe on trestles to give it an even rate of descent down the cliffs to the river from farmlands two thousand feet up on the bench.

The Keane family hauled sacked wheat to the upper end of the pipe, opened the sacks and dumped the wheat. A crew at the bottom filled sacks and sewed them up again for loading on steamboats. The pipe handled up to a thousand sacks a day.

The pipe operated until 1941 when fire burned much of the trestle. By that time trucks were hauling bulk grain and there was no point in rebuilding.

The "wheat pipe" lives only at the Rocky Reach Museum which displays sections of the original pipe.

Another product of early-day ingenuity was the Waterville Tramway that went into operation in the fall of 1902. A series of buckets on a cable, it carried sacked wheat down to a river landing from the wheat-growing plateau 2,400 feet above.

On the return trip up the 9,200-foot cable, the buckets were loaded with lumber, coal, hardware, cement and, occasionally, people. The Tramway is said to have hauled 1,600 sacks of wheat down and eight tons of coal up daily at its peak of operation.

The railroad reached Waterville in 1910, spelling the end of the Tramway. It sat unused until its wooden supports decayed and it collapsed.

The Rocky Reach Museum sent a helicopter to lift two of the Tramway buckets out of a rugged canyon and they also are on display.

A Northwesterner in the Far East

Taiwan

I WAS IN TAIWAN for the *Seattle Times* in 1978. As you may remember, the Republic of China's government and army fled to the island of Taiwan in late 1949 as the Communist Party led by Mao Zedong conquered mainland China and renamed it the People's Republic of China.

For years, the Nationalist Party on Taiwan led by Chiang-kai-shek vowed to launch an invasion from Taiwan to reconquer the rest of China. Those years were a time of tension between the two Chinas with occasional raids and coastal shelling. Martial law, which the government of Taiwan had occasionally used to suppress dissention, was still in effect when I was there, but I saw no visible signs in the streets. It was finally lifted in 1987.

The Republic of China (Taiwan) still considers itself the ruler of all China, but politicians no longer talk about attempting to take it back. In fact, as I write this, increasing trade and tourist visits between the two Chinas continue to decrease tensions.

❖   ❖   ❖

The bones in the museum in Taipei were not particularly eye-catching—some of them almost flat, about the size of a small plate, cracked with some odd scratches on them, a yellowish white color.

But I was impressed, really impressed. I was looking at some of the earliest examples of Chinese writing, indeed of earliest human writing, something like 4,000 years old. These were the famous oracle bones displayed in the National Palace Museum in Taipei.

Take a few seconds to think about life without writing, without the means to record what you've said or heard, to communicate with anyone out of earshot, or jot down something you want to remember. It's probably safe to say that civilization is possible because humans developed the ability to write.

Old bones like the ones I was looking at in the museum had been found by farmers in North China for centuries. They called them "dragon bones" and usually reburied them. Sometimes druggists would buy the bones and grind them up for medicine, used mostly for healing cuts and wounds.

By the 1920s and '30s scientists began to realize that the strange carvings on the bones were ancient examples of writing. The bones were scapular (shoulder) bones from oxen or big turtle shells. And the name "oracle?" Well, that was what modern scientists began calling them when they realized how the ancients had used them.

The ancient scholars used the bones to seek divine guidance. They carved symbols into the bone asking questions. They drilled shallow pits in the back of the bone to facilitate cracking and then applied heat to the bone. The resulting cracks were considered a message from the divine.

A young museum attendant who had spotted me when I walked in (easy; I was the only Caucasian in the place and a head taller than anyone else) told me that some of the characters still had not been deciphered. But of those that had, some are so similar to present-day writing that they can be understood by modern Chinese.

And she drew in my notebook old and new symbols for such ideas as sun, moon, water, tree and forest. She must have explained those oracle bones hundreds of times but she still seemed excited as she told me about them.

❧   ❧   ❧

Walk down Chungwha Road about a mile, my friend told me, get a few blocks off the main drag and "you will see China as it was centuries ago." He was directing me to one of the major markets in Taipei, a labyrinth of narrow alleys packed with stalls selling almost everything the Chinese need for everyday life.

As I walked into the market, the roar of traffic suddenly disappeared, replaced by the shouts of vendors, the shuffling of many feet in the narrow passageways, the occasional squawk of a chicken and, somewhere, a scratchy record playing one of those plaintive (to Western ears) Chinese tunes.

It really was China, probably the quickest transition from modern to old I'd ever seen. But not China as it was centuries ago. For one thing, motorbikes occasionally snorted through the narrow walkways, with the drivers parking in front of the stall where they shopped. And most shoppers dressed in Western style. The exceptions, mostly older women, wore the traditional pajama-like garb of China.

I was there in early morning and catfish were still flopping in bins where they'd been dumped. Smaller fish I couldn't identify swam in ice-cooled tubs of water.

There were live chickens in cages. A woman shopper pointed at one. The peddler held up what looked like a Rhode Island Red for closer inspection. The shopper grabbed the legs herself, hefted it and then nodded.

The vendor stuck the chicken in the head with a small knife, plunged it into a big pot of boiling water and then plucked the feathers. The shopper walked away with a chicken that hadn't been dead more than a few minutes.

As I walked deeper and deeper into the market, I almost wished I had brought my compass from home. But by mentally keeping directions I eventually found my way out without difficulty.

It was a friendly place and I enjoyed being there even if I didn't buy anything. People would grin understandingly when I had to bend under low ceilings that most Chinese wouldn't even notice.

As I emerged from one of the tunnel-like alleys into a busy street, I caught that lonely Chinese tune. Even on a scratchy record, it gave me a tug. I hated to leave.

❧   ❧   ❧

Another time I was haggling with a street vendor in Taipei. We were squatting in the street where his wares were spread out. A group of eight or ten had gathered to watch the American deal with the vendor. There was even a guy holding a baby.

I wanted some old Chinese coins, the big, heavy ones with square holes in the center. The haggling was going well. The vendor and I took turns writing prices on my notebook and passing it back and forth. We were getting close. The spectators seemed to be taking sides with some supporting me and some the vendor.

Then a member of the audience stepped forward and, in good English, asked: "Are you interested in those coins?" He introduced himself as Skinny Y.C. Yang, chief purser on the ship *Independence.* He was in Taipei while his ship was in Hong Kong.

Skinny told me the peddler goes into the countryside and buys coins, mostly from old people, and then sells them for a good profit in the city. He said the coins were from three to five hundred years old.

With Skinny speeding the negotiations, the vendor and I agreed to a price very near what I'd been holding out for. Like most Americans, I'm not very good at haggling and I probably

The old coin seller, Taipei. *Author photo.*

could have gotten it down a little more. But I like my coins, one of which is holding down papers on my desk as I write.

China

I WAS IN THE PEOPLES REPUBLIC OF CHINA for the *Seattle Times* in December of 1979. It was a time of tension between the Peoples Republic and the Republic of China on Taiwan.

I had been to Taiwan the year before and there was talk that the Peoples Republic would refuse admission to those with a passport bearing a Taiwan stamp. It didn't work out that way. In fact, it was sometimes difficult at the Beijing airport to find officials to examine and stamp my passport.

It was an introduction to the casual, friendly way I was treated during my ten days in the Peoples Republic of China, what we then called Red China.

I was fascinated by the country and its history. But I was enchanted by its people—the students practicing their English slowly, precisely: "I am happy...for the opportunity...to speak with...an American." The little girl who took my hand to lead me to a school program; the young farmer who proudly showed me his invention; the guy who gave me a ride on his bicycle.

Those years were also a time of change in China, changes I was only dimly aware of when I was there. Mao Zedong had been dead for three years. Deng Xiaoping, a reformer, had been chairman of the Communist Party for a year, trying to undo the disastrous results of Mao's programs, such as the Cultural Revolution and the Great Leap Forward.

I witnessed a brief flash of freedom for the Chinese to criticize their government, surprising in that tightly controlled country. It was suppressed days after I saw it.

And I joined the daily thousands of people lining up to visit the tomb of Mao, not only a maker of history but ranking with Hitler and Stalin as among the most evil persons in history.

❧   ❧   ❧

I had spent the afternoon on the train and after dinner I really needed a long walk. I was in Shijiazhuang, a sprawling city of 850,000 a couple of hours out of Beijing. It was December 1979, and fairly cold that evening, but I had a warm jacket so I set out alone, headed for the city's commercial center.

It turned out that this walk had an unexpected, heartwarming ending—something you might not expect at home.

I had walked five or six miles—I was young then—and was headed back to the hotel. I began wondering if I was a traffic hazard. Almost every bicycler who went by me would turn and stare at me, some staring so long I feared they'd run in to something.

One biker coasted past me and then stopped and waited until I caught up. He grinned, said something in Chinese, pointed ahead down the street and then patted the second seat on his bicycle on top of the rear fender. I had seen people riding side-saddle on them. They are strengthened as passenger seats.

He was probably in his 30s and slightly built. I was a head taller and a good deal heavier. Could he manage a big American? But I didn't want to hurt his feelings, and I thought it would be fun to get a ride.

It didn't work at first. I guess my arms and legs were too long and he couldn't get started. We couldn't communicate in words but he signaled me to get off, let him start up and then jump back on. It worked. We were off and away. He rang his bell as we passed other bikers who didn't seem to consider his cargo unusual.

After a while, we came to the corner where I needed to turn to go to my hotel. Without me saying anything, he made the correct turn.

"Good," I said. "You even know where I want to go." I doubt if he understood a word I said but he laughed again. I suppose there was only one hotel in that city where foreigners would be staying.

I began to feel serene as my new friend and I wheeled along the street. I had been impressed earlier by the dignity of the great numbers of bicyclers gliding silently along. Now I was part of it.

We arrived at the hotel—too soon for me. I was enjoying the ride. I hopped off and he came back to shake hands. I said, "Thank you very much." He grinned, pointed down the street and said something, probably, "I live down that way."

As he rode away, he looked back and we waved one more time. I walked up to my room with a warm feeling about this city and its people. I wondered if a foreigner out for a late-night walk in Seattle, as obviously foreign looking as I was in China, would be offered a ride. It seemed unlikely.

I've sometimes wondered if the young man was a security agent keeping an eye on the foreigner. But I really don't think so. I think he was being friendly.

❧   ❧   ❧

Dr. Chu Lei, a cardiologist escorting us around a hospital in a provincial city that was an overnight train ride from Beijing, spotted a scales. And, being a cardiologist, he picked out a member of our group, a rather heavy writer from Los Angeles, and had him weigh himself.

Then, commenting that he was taller than the American, Dr. Chu stepped on the scales. He weighed less! He pointed out good naturedly that the American should watch his weight. Then, flushed with success, he looked around for another "patient," saw me and beckoned me over to the scales.

I went with some misgivings. I was wearing a heavy jacket and hiking boots and was carrying a camera. But when I stepped on the scales, it said 95 kilograms (209 pounds), the same as Dr. Chu had weighed, and I was taller.

Dr. Chu's colleagues began laughing, pounding him on the back and shouting, I suppose, the equivalent of "Now, who's overweight?"

It was all good clean fun. Dr. Chu, very tall for a Chinese, laughed as hard as anyone. When we left, I shook his hand and stood on tiptoe. He roared with laughter and said, "I will always remember you. You are taller than I am."

The hospital visit was surprising in several ways, including the lack of privacy for patients. I wondered how a patient in an American hospital would react if a group of foreigners entered and stared, while a doctor explained the ailments. But here patients watched us stolidly, or stared at the wall. Parents would help pose their children for pictures.

In an outpatient ward, a soldier in Peoples Liberation Army uniform, complete with the red star on his peaked cap, watched us without expression as we walked in. He was sitting on a table with his right pant leg pulled up and three smoking needles sticking out of his knee. That's right. The needles were smoking! "This man has arthritis in his knee," a hospital official told us through an interpreter. "It gets worse during cold weather. He will come here for 10 treatments." Acupuncture, yeah, but why the smoke, I asked.

It turned out the Chinese consider heat an integral part of acupuncture therapy. "The needle conveys heat into the nerve loci of the afflicted knee," the attendant said. In fact, he added, the Chinese words for acupuncture translate roughly to "needle combustion."

☙   ☙   ☙

As a sometimes sentimental American parent, it hit me hard when I realized that No. 5 Municipal Kindergarten in Beijing was a boarding school. Parents leave their children, aged three to six, Monday morning and pick them up Saturday evening.

I wrote in the *Seattle Times*:

My realization that these toddlers spent most of the week away from home occurred just after one of them had absolutely melted my heart. As we approached Municipal Kindergarten No. 5, tiny boys and girls ran to meet us. One adorable little girl took my hand to lead me into the school. That's when I melted.

"This way the parents can go to work without worrying about their children," Mrs. Huang, the assistant director, told us. "Of course, when parents can find the time, they come and visit."

I asked if the children get homesick. "Some of them weep at first," she answered. "By this time of year (it was several months into the school year) it no longer happens very often."

From what I heard elsewhere, the weeping is not always confined to the children. It's not unusual for young mothers to show up at work with red eyes after leaving a toddler at kindergarten on Monday.

Mrs. Huang said the children are taught the Chinese language, music, fine arts, handcraft and physical training. "And, of course, we don't want them to forget to love Chairman Mao, Chairman Hua and the motherland," she added. (Mao had died several years earlier and was succeeded by Hua Guofeng who served as chairman until 1981.) One wall of the kindergarten had portraits of Mao and Hua. Across the room were pictures of Marx, Engels, Lenin and Stalin.

The children honored us with a musical program with songs such as "I Am a Worker," and "I Dreamed I Met Chairman Mao." The atmosphere was much like home. Healthy, animated faces of children proudly going through their pieces. Giggling from the hall where others waited their turn. Grinning teachers leaning in the doorway to watch.

But it seemed too perfect, more accomplished than a typical American elementary school production. As it turned out, it was. I learned that these appealing little children perform for foreign visitors an average of four times a week. And, presumably, run to take the hand of a charmed foreigner.

❧   ❧   ❧

The spirit of democracy flickered briefly in China in 1978 and 1979, ignited by a poet from the countryside who put up posters on a brick wall along an otherwise forgettable street in downtown Beijing.

Democracy Wall, so named by western news correspondents, attracted world attention as it caught on with the Chinese people. The country was recovering from the disastrous rule of Mao Zedong who had died a few years earlier. Hundreds used flour paste to brush large-character posters, many critical of government actions, onto the drab bricks.

The wall, a little more than a block long, shielded the street from a parking lot for transit busses. I walked along it one midnight in December 1979. (Why midnight? I forget, but my knees were better then.) I was surprised to see dozens reading the posters by street lights even in the middle of the night.

I visited the wall again a day later and there were hundreds of men, women, elderly, teenagers. At some of the apparently more interesting posters, there were clusters three or four deep. There wasn't much talk. Most of them were reading silently.

One western correspondent told me he considered the wall the "single most sensitive spot" in Beijing for gauging the public mood. With his interpreter he visited the wall twice a day.

Some of the posted statements, I was told, harshly criticized government policies, particularly those of the Mao era. A year earlier, Deng Xiaoping, China's vice premier who was working to reverse some of Mao's disastrous programs, commented on the wall, saying it was good for the people to have a place to express opinions.

But as it turned out, I saw the wall just a few days before it was suppressed by the Communist Party. Despite Deng's favorable comment, Democracy Wall became another frustrated attempt for political freedom by the Chinese people. New posters at the wall were banned.

I wrote in the *Seattle Times*:

> A few days after my visit old posters were cleaned from the wall. The government designated a small park in Beijing as the new place for posters (freedom to put up posters is guaranteed in China's constitution) but announced that authors and visitors were to sign their names, pseudonyms, addresses and places of work.

Democracy Wall, a brief flicker of political freedom in China—snuffed out, an almost forgotten part of history.

❧   ❧   ❧

There weren't many chances for an American in China in 1979 to speak with regular, ordinary people. The biggest barrier, at least for me, was language.

So I was pleased when Chang Chien-kuo slipped into the bus seat next to me and wondered politely if he could ask some questions about America. He was an interpreter who had been accompanying us for a few days. Chang was 24.

Chang asked about my family and how we lived, about our house and our friends. There weren't any hard questions and none the least hostile.

He wanted to know how many children I had. When I told him we had one girl and four boys, he nodded approvingly and said: "Four sons. Good for you." He asked no further questions about the girl, although I reminded him of our daughter several times.

Does each child have a bathroom in his room? (No.) Do the children get money from you? (A little. Mostly they earn their own money from odd jobs.) Do they give that money to you? (No. It is theirs.)

What do your sons do on Sundays? Do you have contact with their teachers? Can you ask the teachers questions? Are your sons as tall as you are? Do they study foreign languages? What age will your children leave home? Do Americans find wives for their sons?

As I answered, I wondered what Chang was thinking. His face provided few clues except for a few times such as when he asked "Is your wife the same age as you?" (No, she is seven years younger.) He nodded: "That's good." Later, he wondered if my wife's father were retired. (No, I think he's afraid of being bored if he retires.) Another nod of approval.

I threw in questions of my own. What do Chang's friends ask him about the Americans he meets on the job? He thought a moment and then, "They ask me, 'Can they afford a car?' They think Americans are very rich."

Would Chang be allowed to own a car? "No, and I wouldn't want to." (In the years since, of course, car ownership has become widespread in China. The country has become a major market for the automobile industry.)

What is Chang asked most often by foreign visitors to China? The answer was prompt: "The No. 1 question is about sexual freedom in China." What does he answer? "There isn't any."

Then Chang resumed his questioning: When you get home, who will meet you at the airport? (My wife.) In your car? (Yes.) How many cars do you have? (One.) How do you get to work? (Bus.) What is the bus fare? (Sixty cents each way.)

Who cooks at your house? Do you do the washing by hand or do you have a machine? Does your house have central heating? Do you have other people to your house and do you visit in other houses?

It was my turn again: Was Chang sent to the country to work on farms as so many young city people were in past years? (No. There were four children in my family in Beijing. Two were assigned to work in the country. My sister and I were given special training—Chang in languages and his sister in a technical field for a job in a synthetics factory.) (Chang's family preceded China's controversial one-child policy.)

I asked if he enjoyed the foreigners he met on the job. "Yes, most of them. But I don't like people from Singapore. They are too critical."

Chang wondered if our children ever wore clothing from other families. (Hand-me-downs? Sure. Neighbors and relatives often pass along outgrown children's clothing that still has wear in it.)

Chang wrote "hand-me-downs" in a notebook he calls "Book of Slangs."

But it was the subject of spanking that seemed to interest Chang the most. He asked: Do you spank your children? (Yes, when they need it.) Who gives the spankings? (Sometimes my wife, but mostly I do.) Were you spanked as a boy? (Yes, when I needed it.)

Most Chinese parents do not spank their children and schools discourage it, preferring "reasoning" as a disciplinary method.

The bus ride ended while we were still talking. He sought me out the next day to ask more questions about spanking.

How do you do it? Do you make them lie down? Do you use anything besides your hand?

How long do you beat them? (We call it spanking, Chang. It depends. Usually just a few spanks.) Do they cry? How long? Afterwards, do they stand away from you and refuse to talk to you?

How many times a year do you beat them? (Spank, Chang. Perhaps an average of three or four times a year.) At age 16, do you still beat them? (No. If you still need to spank a 16-year-old, you are in real trouble.)

The final question was on another subject: Do American mothers think they can teach children best and don't want their children to go to kindergarten for fear they will become just like all other children?

I had to admit I do not know any American mothers who feel that way.

Chang gave me his mail address. I sent him a copy of my story hoping it wouldn't get him in trouble in the tightly controlled China of 1979.

❧   ❧   ❧

I may be a city boy, but I've been on farms off and on all my life, farms owned by uncles, cousins, friends. So I was interested that winter day in 1979 when I arrived at the Dong An Cheng Production Brigade, part of a farm commune in central China. There were people all over the place.

Not all of them were doing anything except staring at the foreigner, me. But a lot of work actually was getting done by both men and women—using horses, two-wheel carts, pitchforks, shovels, wheelbarrows. Women? Yeah. A woman swinging a pick was part of a crew of four digging a ditch for winter seed storage.

But what struck me was how many workers there were for a specific job.

In 1979 there were still more Chinese living in the country than in cities. But China in the late 1970s was changing in ways I was only dimly aware of when I was there. Deng Xiaoping, China's vice premier at the time, had begun economic reforms that started the Chinese economy on its way to where, today, it is one of the world's largest. The reforms created jobs in the cities, lifting millions out of poverty and triggering one of the greatest internal migrations in history as millions upon millions of farm workers moved to cities seeking jobs and a better life.

By 2012, more than 30 years after I was there, population in China's cities surpassed that of the countryside.

The Dong An Cheng Production Brigade was doing well, we were told as we sat in a big room with windows all along one side, through which the sun streamed. The room seemed out of place, even on a big farm. I decided its most frequent use was for political indoctrinations for the brigade's workers.

I wrote in the *Seattle Times*:

"Before liberation (in 1949) this was a poor village, often flooded," the brigade's director began, with frequent pauses for the interpreter. "There were 14 landlords in our village and they owned half the land. Much of the area was not planted. Irrigation was spotty and poor.

"The peasants did not have enough food or clothing in those days. There were 37 households working for the landlords. Another 137 households could find only seasonal work and were unemployed the rest of the year."

(It struck me odd that industrial employees in the cities were referred to as "workers," while those on the farm were "peasants." There did not seem to be a social distinction.)

"Another 24 households went begging outside. Sixteen brothers and sisters died as beggars.

"After liberation, under the leadership of the party and Chairman Mao, our poor peasants became masters of the state, overthrew the landlords and got the land from their hands.

"We made the land level. We planted many trees and turned wasted land into good land. Following Chairman Mao's call, we engaged in capital construction, digging wells, building water-storage ponds and irrigation systems."

OK, it was propaganda, but fairly mild as propaganda goes. And it was backed up by the prosperous look and neatness of the commune. It produced wheat, apples (I ate one, crisp and delicious), pears, and vegetables as well as cattle, chickens, rabbits, pond fish, and mink.

Mink, in the Peoples Republic? "Strictly for export," he answered. "Cash crop, at $50 a pelt, more than 100 a year."

He did not mention some of the drastic, disastrous programs tried under Mao and abandoned. But he did say there had been a change in who makes policy decisions for the communes.

Far-off bureaucrats who probably had never raised a blister from real work no longer were making policy decisions for the communes, including this one. Those decisions now were made at the brigade level by people who do the work, or at least who talk to the workers—er, peasants. Communes had been taking over policy making on their own in the 1970s, independent actions apparently tolerated by the central government. The government made the change official in the early 1980s.

"Every family in this brigade now has enough food," [the briefing continued]. "Every family has a (savings) deposit in the bank. There is a cooperative medical station run by the brigade. Since 1976, members have been able to go to the clinic without paying. Children go to a free middle school. Haircuts are free."

Dong An Cheng Production Brigade in 1979 numbered 2,393 persons in 537 households, an average of a little more than 4.5 persons a household.

I didn't see any tractors but the brigade said it owned six of them, plus five trucks, 24 small tractors (I assumed the little three-wheel jobs) and 48 electric motors.

Except for machinery and electricity, the brigade produced just about everything it needed. It had manufactured more than three miles of concrete water pipe, half of which was underground. The farm could produce four tons of cement a day, its brick factory 30,000 bricks a day. We saw row on row of concrete pigsties, hundreds of them.

There was even room for innovation in this huge, regimented operation. One of the "peasants" proudly showed me an automatic feed-dispensing device in a pig shed. Powered by a small electric motor, it ran on a track between rows of stalls and also pumped feed into an underground pipe leading to another shed. It was simple, obviously homemade, effective and ingenious.

As we left, we drove blacktop lanes lined with slender poplars and spotted frequently with basketball backboards. Brick warehouses and concrete posts around a cow pasture contrasted with a chicken pen made of bamboo. Even here on the farm, men and women with brooms kept the ground almost bare of leaves and litter.

I'm sure that farms like the Dong An Cheng Brigade now have fewer workers per job than the numbers that surprised me long ago. But I'll bet men and women with brooms still keep the ground clean and unlittered.

(I had previously noticed the ratio of workers to jobs in Chinese cities. For example, in railroad yards where switch engines would be making up trains, you'd see two or maybe three smiling young men sitting on the locomotive's "bumper," what I call the cow-catcher. Two or three guys for one job.)

❧   ❧   ❧

I was visiting a farm home and all the chairs were taken so I sat on the kang, the traditional heated bed of rural China. For my money, the kang is one of the most ingenious of the long line of Chinese inventions. It is a king-size brick box heated by a small, coal-burning stove at one side.

The heat is gentle. It took a few minutes before I could feel the heat where I sat. The stove keeps the bricks warm all night.

Kangs typically are big. This one was about six feet wide and ran the length of the room, about ten feet.

An entire family could snuggle down on one during a cold night. In fact, Mao Zedong wrote that he once shared a kang with seven other students during a bitter winter.

"When we were all packed fast on the kang, there was scarcely room for any of us to breathe," Mao wrote. "I used to have to warn people on each side of me when I wanted to turn over."

The family I was visiting was not that crowded. They had two kangs for four people.

Many Chinese farm families use the kang as a table during the day. With a mat spread over the kang, they sit cross-legged on the warm platform for a meal.

Useful. But it must make a VERY hard bed.

Mrs. Li Chihua, our hostess, had taken time off from her job in the commune's vegetable fields to talk to us.

Her home was as neat as a pin. I looked in vain for a speck of dust. At one point, Mrs. Li stopped talking and motioned sternly at the interpreter to stop dropping cigarette ashes on her cooking stove. The cooking space was very small. The toilet was outside.

Mrs. Li stood in the courtyard to tell us good-bye as we left. I thanked her for her hospitality and told her I thought she had a nice house.

"Thank you," she answered. "Of course, living standards are much higher in your country."

❧   ❧   ❧

The Peoples Republic of China in 1979 was a place where an American would attract a crowd, just by being there, particularly in the smaller cities. If you stopped to buy something, the observers pressed up close, the curiosity becoming intense.

If you were in a car stopped for traffic, the windows would be filled with staring faces.

And it was a place where some of my preconceived ideas crumbled. In the past, I'd thought of the Peoples Liberation Army as the hordes of "volunteers" who streamed across the Yalu River in the Korean war.

Now my mental picture of the P.L.A. is of soldiers hanging out the windows of a railroad troop car at a whistle stop. Spotting foreigners in a nearby train, more and more heads thrust out of windows and doors—red stars on their caps, red patches on their collars—as they crowded each other to wave and grin. They looked so young.

And there was the soldier leading a tiny boy by the hand at a museum in Beijing. The boy had a red star sewed on his cap.

❧   ❧   ❧

We were visiting Mrs. Chung in her apartment in a city several hours from Beijing. One of the newswomen in our group asked who does the cooking for the family.

Mrs. Chung, who worked at Cotton Mill No. 1 across the street, answered, "It depends on who gets home first."

Does your husband cook? Answer: "Yes, sometimes. It is the habit in China. Men and women are equal and cooking is not necessarily a woman's job."

There was a short pause, and then Mrs. Chung added with a faint smile: "But women cook more."

I asked what fuel they used for cooking. Mrs. Chung took me out to the kitchen and lifted a tea kettle off the stove to show me a glowing briquette. It was about the shape of a one-pound coffee can and had holes in it to accelerate burning.

I had seen similar briquettes being hauled around town on bicycle-pulled carts. Others were stacked on balconies and in hallways.

Our visit was in winter and Mrs. Chung told me they cooked with gas in the summer when the stove's heat was not needed to help warm the apartment.

Mrs. Chung's kitchen was tiny, like those in many American apartments. There was some counter space but not much. The sink was concrete. There was no refrigerator but glass-paneled doors at one end of the kitchen opened to a pantry that probably served as a cooler in the winter.

❧   ❧   ❧

A middle-aged Chinese man named Seedling of the Revolution, if he's still alive, may be trying to adopt a child orphaned in the great earthquake that hit China's Sichuan Province recently. He himself was orphaned in the even more deadly quake that destroyed Tangshan in 1976, killing an estimated 242,000 and injuring 160,000.

So how did Seedling of the Revolution acquire that awkward, relentlessly patriotic name? He and more than 500 other orphans from Tangshan were sent to an orphanage in Shijiazhuang, capital city of Hebei Province in northeastern China. These were the kids who, for one reason or another, couldn't be placed with relatives and the government ruled out adoption for most of those remaining. They were, in effect, children of the Communist Party. Seedling of the Revolution was one of many children who could not be identified by family and was given a patriotic name.

I was in Shijiazhuang on another assignment for the *Times* in December 1979, when I learned of the Tangshan orphans. By then, a little more than three years after the quake, the number was dwindling slowly as children became old enough to join the work force.

I don't know why Shijiazhuang was selected for the orphanage except that it was in the same part of China as Tangshan. The government moved quickly, as totalitarian ones sometimes do. The orphanage buildings went up in 15 days.

Some of the children understandably had mental problems from the terror of the earthquake, the loss of family, and being uprooted to a strange new place. The orphanage drew teaching specialists from around the country, we were told.

The city took the children to heart. Townspeople visited often and on holidays brought fruit and gifts. Visitors were sometimes greeted by children singing Chinese words (I don't know what the words meant) to the tune of "Oh, Susannah."

The Tangshan quake, at 3:42 A.M. July 28, 1976, was a surprise to Chinese geologists. It occurred far from the earthquake-prone southwest where the Indian-Australian Plate is thrusting beneath the Eurasian Plate, pushing up the Himalaya Mountains.

As it turned out there was a right-lateral, strike-slip fault running right under Tangshan, a city of about one million at that time. Horizontal displacement during the quake was as much as five feet. That means that if you were standing on one side of the fault at the time of the earthquake, real estate on the other side would jump five feet to your right, within seconds.

Tangshan is a coal-mining city and there were 2,200 miners underground when the quake struck. A few died when structures fell on them, but almost all those underground survived. Some 1,900 miners did die—they were at home asleep when the quake hit. Most of the houses were brick, with concrete roofs, and they were flattened.

The Tangshan quake had an estimated magnitude of 7.8, a really big one. Adding to the horror, an aftershock almost as powerful struck 16 hours later, killing many who were awaiting rescue in the rubble.

The Tangshan orphans had toured their rebuilding city just a year before I was there. We were told it was "inconvenient" for foreigners to visit. But Tangshan has been rebuilt and is advertising itself as a tourist destination.

Seedling of the Revolution, the Tangshan orphan, may be back in his native city. And he may well be using a less cumbersome name by now.

❧   ❧   ❧

We left the hazy, early morning sunlight and stepped into a huge, red-carpeted entry room. Facing us was a stark-white, three-times-life-size statue of Mao Zedong—seated, legs crossed, hands on the chair arms, a slight smile. The statue seemed to be floating against a vast tapestry of misty mountains, valleys, streams. There was a feeling of depth, as though you were looking beyond Mao into China.

This was the Mao Mausoleum at Tiananmen Square in Beijing, the tomb of a man who had changed the world. In 40 years, he had literally wrenched China from a backward country long dominated by Western nations, and set it on the track toward world power. Along with his successes, he made disastrous decisions. He was responsible for millions of deaths—of his own people—by starvation or execution. With mixed emotions I approached the room where his body had been on view since his death in 1976, just three years earlier.

And I wondered what all those people waiting patiently in line outside thought as a small group of American journalists was moved to the head of the line. There were thousands—men, women, children, senior citizens—waiting to visit the tomb. I even saw a baby in a stroller. I couldn't tell who was doing the organizing but you'd see a double line of people marching along to join a bigger group, a square of maybe 200 persons. That human square would feed into a four-abreast line entering the mausoleum. It was open only half of the day, and they told us they put 10,000 visitors through each day. So maybe the regimented crowd-handling was necessary. But I couldn't help wondering how a crowd of Americans would react. There were no sarcastic comments or even dirty looks—just passive stares—as we foreigners were moved to the head of the line and into the mausoleum.

There was no talking in the entry room. The red carpet deadened sound as we split into two lines around the statue, one to the left, one to the right.

"Take off your heads," our interpreter whispered. We assumed he meant "hats," and complied. We had already been told to leave behind cameras, handbags, purses.

We moved to the next room that was dominated by a big bier surrounded by flowers. The flowers were so perfect I wondered if they were plastic. But they told us they were fresh, flown here daily from all over China.

We walked slowly past Mao's embalmed body that is in an airless space beneath a glass cover. His face looked like yellow parchment, drawn and tired. But there was no mistaking that face.

The sleeves of the grey, Mao jacket extending down his sides looked flat, empty.

China's flag, a red field with yellow hammer and sickle, covered the body's chest. Mao was one of the heroic leaders of the legendary Long March in 1934, and the revered leader of Red China until his death.

Without words in that hushed space we kept moving. No stopping to stare. As we stepped into another room, a Canadian woman in our group whispered: "God, I'm shaken." I wasn't shaken, but I did feel I had seen the body of a man who had changed history.

As I write this more than 30 years later, I learn that Chinese still line up each day to visit Mao's tomb and that daily attendance is still 10,000 in the half day it is open. It's difficult for an American to understand the continued devotion to this leader as his mixed legacy—both heroic and horrifying—has become more fully known.

Japan and World War II

DURING WORLD WAR II a horrific human tragedy occurred on Saipan Island. In 1978 I visited Suicide Cliff on the island, and wrote this for the *Seattle Times*:

It is peaceful now at this beautiful spot on Saipan's rugged coastline, a few miles north of popular tourist beaches. There is only the sound of the sea smashing against rocky cliffs. But this was the scene of one of history's most heart-wrenching human tragedies.

It occurred near the end of the American conquest of this strategic island in July, 1944. After some of the toughest fighting anywhere in the Pacific during World War II, the Americans controlled most of the island.

The Japanese military force and several thousand civilians had been pushed into a pocket here.

Then it began. Horrified Americans saw Japanese soldiers and civilians alike begin throwing themselves off the cliff, seeking an honorable death in preference to capture.

Some families lined up facing the ocean cliff and were pushed off one by one. When the father was the only one left, he would turn and run backwards over the cliff.

Again and again. By the hundreds. Some even say thousands jumped that day. The fall, perhaps 80 feet, was bad enough. But the boiling sea sucked down those who weren't killed immediately.

American ships hurriedly launched rescue boats. They rigged up loudspeakers that blared in Japanese, "Don't jump!" But the mass suicides continued.

A few American marines arrived on the cliff from the land side and tried to stop the self-destruction. The Japanese civilians fought them off. Some families would cluster around a hand grenade, and the father would pull the pin.

Americans on both ships and on land, even though hardened by weeks of battle, often were unable to watch. Sickened, they turned away.

There weren't many survivors among those who tried to kill themselves that terrible day. But a few did survive, were captured, and finally got back to Japan.

Occasionally, one of those survivors would show up among the planeloads of Japanese tourists who visited Saipan after the war.

❧   ❧   ❧

Mary Lou and I spent a month in Japan after I retired in 1991. Our home base was Nagoya, where we stayed with our daughter, Mary, her husband Joe Prall, an engineer on Boeing assignment, and their son Mike, almost two years old.

One day we visited Hiroshima, and a surprisingly haunting feeling consumed me. Things in my life were coming full circle.

I had worked at Hanford where ammunition for the second atomic bomb dropped on Japan had been manufactured. I had witnessed a Hiroshima-size atomic bomb explode in Nevada. I'd worked in the Pacific Testing Ground, seen the devastation, and talked to the people displaced by America's testing of 59 nuclear devices over 12 years. I had visited the field on Tinian Island where a B-29 had taken off in 1945, loaded with the bomb bound for Hiroshima. And now I was in the first city struck by a nuclear bomb, standing at Ground Zero. It was deeply moving, a piece of history I might not have chosen.

The Hiroshima Peace Memorial. This cenotaph contains the names of all the people who died on August 6, 1945. *Author photo.*

Some of the museum's displays were heart-wrenching. There was a tricycle ridden by a 3-year-old boy who died of blast injuries three days later. His father buried him in their back yard with the trike so he wouldn't be lonely. His body was moved to a cemetery later, and the trike donated to the museum.

I'll never forget the story of a young girl who developed leukemia after the bombing. She believed she would be restored to health if she made a thousand paper cranes. She had completed 954 when she died several years after the blast. Her statue is in a park near the museum.

I'd wondered whether Japanese visitors to the Hiroshima museum with its horrifying displays would resent the presence of an American of obviously World War II age. Would older visitors react differently than the young for whom the war was distant history?

Reactions were about what you might expect at home. The young, like young people everywhere, were friendly but engrossed with their own group. The older people, grey-haired like me, were outgoing and friendly, smiling, and bowing when we met. I was relieved and a little surprised. The world had changed unbelievably fast during the 20th century.

I looked back at my life that day and realized how privileged I had been in my career as a news reporter. This lanky grandson of Northwest pioneers lived through an age of scientific, medical and cultural developments that my parents couldn't have imagined, and I had experienced much of it first hand. Not only did I get to walk in the crater at Mount St. Helens and watch a nuclear bomb detonated, I had met scientists, doctors and ordinary folks in many nations. And I got to tell their stories in the pages of the newspaper. I have been so lucky.

Index

Page numbers in italics indicate photographs

Admiral Oriental Line, 102
Albany, OR, 94
Algeria, 65
Anchorage, AK, 56
Anjain, Lekoj, 74-75
Army Corps of Engineers, 116
Arthur, Pres. Chester A., 99
Atomic Energy Commission, 31-32, 67; Marshall Islands recovery study sponsored by, 71-75
Atomic Man, *see* McCluskey, Harold
Auberton, Don, 132

Balto (sled dog), 56
Beck, Dave, 15
Behrens, Grew W., 131-33
Beijing, China, 146, 147, 150-52, 161, 164-66
Bellevue, WA, 52, 53
Berlin Blockade (1948), *see* Cold War
Bickleton, WA, 137-38
Bikini Atoll, Marshall Islands, 71-74
Blue Mountains, 66
Bonneville Dam, 111
Breitenstein, Dr. Bryce, 58-60
Brewer, Howard
Bridge of the Gods, 112, 113
Broughton, Lt. William, 117

Cairo, Egypt, 65
Camp Kilmer, NJ, 64
Cape Flattery, 50
Cape Mendocino, WA, 100
Carson, Rachel, 44
Carter, Pres. Jimmy, 128
Cascade Range, 24, 35, 66, 80, 87, 88, 112, 120, 124, 134
Cascades of the Columbia, *see* Columbia River

Casey, Zane, 12
Celilo Falls, *see* Columbia River
Chang Chien-kuo, 153-55
Cheney-Palouse Tract, 90
Cherry Valley, WA, 53
Chiang-kai-shek, 141
Chicago, IL, 7
China (People's Republic of China), plutonium fallout from, 121; touring, 146-66
Chu Lei, Dr., 148-49
Chung, Mrs., 161-62
Clark Fork River, 89
Clark, William, 111-12, 117
Clinton, Gordon S., 65
Cold War, 61-77; Hanford's role in, 121, 127
Colfax, WA, 88, 135
Columbia Basin Irrigation Project, 121-24
Columbia Basin News, 32
Columbia Basin, WA, 87-88, 121-24; sand dunes, 124-25; juniper trees, 125
Columbia Gorge, 87
Columbia River, 3, 7, 12, 16, 25, 61, 66, 83, 87, 88, 94, 102, 126, 135, 138; Columbia River natural history and Cascades of the Columbia, 111-13; Celilo Falls, 113-16; Homely Rapids, 116-19; Umatilla Rapids, 116-19, dams and irrigation, 119-20; geologic history, 120; radioactivity impact on, 120-21; irrigation projects, 121-24; basalt flows, 135; Gallery of the Columbia Museum at Rocky Reach Dam, 138-40
Colville Tribe, 132

Communist Party (China), 141, 146, 162
Connell, WA, 24
Coos Bay, OR, 103, 106
Cowen, John M., 103
Crater Lake, 135
Croes, Dale, 50
Cuban Missile Crisis (1962), *see* Cold War
Cultural Revolution (China), 146

Darwin, Charles, 79
Deng Xiaoping, 146, 152, 156
Dion, Larry, 29
Donaldson, Dr. Lauren R., 53-55
Dong An Cheng Production Brigade, 156-59
Douglas County, WA, 3
Duclos, Al, 14
Dusty, WA, 135
Duvall, WA, 53

Edmondson, W. Thomas, 43-44
Edwards, John, 133
Eisenhower, Pres. Dwight D., 64-65
Elko, NV, 7
Eniwetak Atoll, Marshall Islands, 71-73
Ephrata, WA, 2
Eppeson, James R., 105
Eurasian (tectonic) Plate, 163

Fairfield, Clara, 94
"The Farmer's Wife," *see* Tampien, Beth and George
Foley, Katie, 52
Franklin County, WA, 88, 123

Gallery of the Columbia Museum, 138-40
General Electric Company, 32
Gilbert, Greg, 92
Gillum, Billy, 124
Gillum, O. C., 124
Glomar Challenger, 83-85

Grand Coulee Dam, 121, 123, 136
Grant County, WA, 3
Grants Pass, OR, 29
Great Britain, 65
Great Depression, 9, 13, 24
Great Northern Railway, 1, 2
Grenfell, Rear Admiral E. W., 108
Groton, CT, 108
Gulf of Tonkin Incident, 76-77

Hanford High School, 126-27
Hanford Nuclear Reservation, 29, 31-32, 58, 60, 61, 120-21, 126-28, 168
Hebei Province, China, 162
Himalaya Mountains, 163
Hiroshima Peace Memorial, *169*-70
Hiroshima, 168-70
Hoh River, 129
Hoko River, 49
Homely Rapids, *see* Columbia River
Hooper, Peter, 79
Horrigan, Judge B. B., 123
Horse Heaven Hills, 137
Hua Guofeng, 150
Hughes, Mike, 15
Hungarian uprising (1956), *see* Cold War
Hydrogen bomb, 72, 74

Ides, Harold, 49-51
Ides, Isabell, 51
Ides, Jack and Fanny, 50
Ides, John, 50-51
Iditarod Race, 57
Indian-Australian (tectonic) Plate, 163
Intrepid (Coast Guard boat), 103-6
Iowa City, IA, 7

Jackson, Senator Henry W., 108
James Island, WA, 15, 16
Japan, 74, 102, 167-70
Johannes (Eniwetak Atoll leader), 73
Johnson, Pres. Lyndon B., 76

Johnson, Tex, 63
Johnson, Tom, 97-98
Johnston, David, 97
Juan de Fuca (tectonic) Plate, 79
Juda (Bikini Atoll leader), 73-74
Jump-Off Joe, 7-8

Kahlotus, WA, 24
Kalaloch, WA, 82
Kamiak Butte, 79-82
Katmai, *see* volcanic eruptions
Keane, James E., 139
Kennewick Courier-Reporter, 24-26
Kennewick, WA, 7, 12, 13, 14, 25, 52
Kiel, Dr. William, 41-42
Kiel, Willie, 41-42
Kili Island, Marshall Islands, 73-74
Knight, James H., 7
Korosec, Mike, 95-96
Krakatoa, *see* volcanic eruptions
Kulm, Dr. Lavern D., 83

Lake Ozette, 130
Lake Union, 101
Lake Washington, 42-44
LaPush, WA, 15, 128, 129
Lester, Bill ("Ranger Bill"), 130
Lewis and Clark, 111, 115, 117
Liddell, Pete, 131
Light House Service, 100
Linotype machines, *20*, 21, 25, 36-39
Lipke, Fred, 39-40
Livingston, TX, 85
Locust Grove, 10-11
Long Island Sound, 108
Los Angeles, CA, 148
Luce, Henry, 29-30

Makah Tribe, 49-51, 99
Malaya, 65
Manhattan Project, 126
Manzanita, WA, 94
Mao Zedung, 141, 146, 150-51, 152, 157, 160; tomb (mausoleum) of, 147, 164-66

Marshall, Frank, 39-41
Martin, Robert "Pepper," 10
McClelland, Lindsay, 133
McCluskey, Harold, 58-60
McNary Dam, 12, 117, *118*, 119
McNeil, Charles, 85
Mid-Columbia Library, Kennewick, 52
Missoula, MT, 89
Mount Adams, 94
Mount Hood, 94, 117
Mount Mazama, 134
Mount Rainier, 94, 133
Mount Si, 134
Mount St. Helens, 89, 135; Timberline Camp, 91-92, 95; Goat Rocks, 91; Harry Truman, 92-95; eruption, 94; sound of eruption, 94-95; crater exploration, 95-97, 170; death of David Johnston, 97
Museum of History and Industry (Seattle), 29

N Reactor (Hanford Nuclear Reservation), 127
Nagoya, Japan, 168
Nasser, Abdul, 65
National Palace Museum, Tapei, Taiwan, 142
National Science Foundation, 84
Nationalist Party (Taiwan), 141
Nautilus (submarine), 106-9
Neah Bay, WA, 49-51, 100
Nevada nuclear testing (1952), 65-70, 168
New York City, NY, 7, 56
New York *Sun Times*, 56
Niagara Falls, NY, 91
Nome, AK, 55-57
North American (tectonic) Plate, 79
North Bend, WA, 134
North Platte, NE, 7
North Pole, 108
Northern Pacific Railway, 12
Norton Sound, AK, 56

Olympia, WA, 94
Olympic National Park, 128
Olympic Peninsula, 15, 130
Omaha, NE, 7
Oregon coast, 83-84
Oregon State University, 83
Oregon Trail, 41-42, 66-67, 70
Oysterville, WA, 94
Ozette, WA, 99

Pacific (Nuclear) Testing Ground, 168
Palouse Country (Palouse Hills), 3-5,
    80, 85-88, 89-90
Palouse Falls, 88-91
Palouse River, 90
Pasco Basin, 87, 88
Pasco Chamber of Commerce, 9
Pasco Herald, 4, 10, 19, *23,* 24, 25
Pasco Hotel, 11
Pasco Irrigation Block 1, *see*
    Columbia Basin Irrigation Project
Pasco, WA, 7, 9, 12, 13, 14, 113, 122
Patty, Stan, 98
Pend Oreille Lake, 89
People's Republic of China, *see* China
Peoples Liberation Army (China),
    149, 161
Plate tectonics, 79-85; *see also*
    Eurasian Plate, Indian-Australian
    Plate
Plunkett, Bill, 35
Portland, OR, 94
Potholes Canal, 124
Powell, Robert, 82
Prall, Joe and Mary, 168
Prall, Mike, 168
Puget Sound, xi, 106
Pugnetti, Don, 30
Pullman, WA, 4, 5, 80, 122, 135

Quillayute River, 15-18
Quincy Flats, WA, 3
Quincy, WA, 122

Rau, Weldon, 82
Raymond, WA, 41

Reddin, Johnny, 36
Reed, Jim, 25, 26
Reed, Ralph E., 25
Rehberg, John C., 105
Republic of China, *see* Taiwan
Richland Library, 52
Richland, WA, 12, 29-32, 51, 62
Rockwell, Norman, 11
Rocky Mountains, 87, 120
Rocky Reach Dam, 138
Rocky Reach Museum, *see* Gallery of
    the Columbia Museum
Rongela Atoll, Marshall Islands,
    74-75

Sacajawea State Park, Pasco, WA, 12
Sackit Canyon, 81-82
Saddle Mountains, 61
San Francisco, CA, 7, 66, 101
San Juan Islands, WA, 94
Santa Barbara, CA, 44
Saturday Evening Post, 11-12
Scully, Roy, 58, 100, 102, 126, 127
Seattle Times, xi, 10, 29; typesetting,
    36-39; columns and stories in,
    39-41, 41-42, 42-44, 44-47, 49-51,
    51-53, 53-55, 55-57, 58-60, 62-63,
    63-65, 74-75, 79-85, 85-92, 91-94,
    95-97, 97, 99-103, 103-6, 106-9,
    111-13, 113-16, 126-28, 128-30,
    131-32, 133-34, 137-38, 143-45,
    150-51, 151-52, 156-59, 162-64,
    167-68
Seattle, WA, 35, 43, 101, 137, 148;
    boarding houses, 35-36; receiving
    Hungarian refugees, 63-65
Seppala, Leonhard, 55-57
Service, Robert, 25
Shaw, David, 32
Sheviakov, Yuri, 63
Shi Shi Beach, WA, 128
Shijiazhuang, China, 147, 162-63
Sichuan Province, China, 162
Silent Spring (book), 44
Skartland, Olav, 13-14

Skill, Bob, 12
Smithsonian Scientific Event Alert
    Network, 133
Snake River, 10, 12, 87, 90, 115
Soviet Union (USSR), 32, 61-65
Speed Graphic camera, 27, *28*, 29-30,
    62
Spirit Lake, WA, 92, 95
Spokane, Portland & Seattle Railway,
    11
Spokane, WA, 2, 89, 136
Strait of Juan de Fuca, 49, 102
Submarine Force Museum, 108
Suez Canal Crisis (1956), 65
Sutherland, Daniel, 103-5
Swiftsure Bank, 102
Swiftsure lightship, 101

Tacoma, WA, xi
Taiwan, 141-45, 146
Tambora, *see* volcanic eruptions
Tampien, Beth and George, 51-53
Tangshan, China, 162-64
Tatoosh Island, 100, 102-3
Teamsters Union, 15
Tectonic plates, *see* Plate tectonics
The Dalles Dam, 113, 116
The Dalles, OR, 94
The Evergreen (newspaper), *see*
    Washington State University
Thompson, Moe, 16
Tiananmen Square, 164
Timberline Camp, *see* Mount St.
    Helens
Time Magazine, 29-30
Tinian Island, 168
Togo (sled dog), 56-57
Trainor, Will, 8
Tri-City Herald, 26-27, 30-32, 51, 62;
    nuclear testing in Nevada, 65-70;
    construction of McNary Dam,
    117-19
Truman, Harry, 92-95
Tuve, Rolf W., 24-25

U.S. Bureau of Land Management,
    125
U.S. Bureau of Reclamation, 123, 131
U.S. Coast Guard, 100-101, 102-6
U.S. Department of Defense, 76
U.S. Geological Survey, 82
U.S. Postal Service, 7
U.S.S. *Constitution* ("Old Ironsides"),
    108-9
U.S.S. *Maddox,* 76
U.S.S. *Ticonderoga,* 76
U.S.S. *Turner Joy,* 76
Ujelang Atoll, Marshall Islands, 73
Umatilla (steamship), 99, 102
Umatilla Lightship, 99-101
Umatilla Rapids, *see* Columbia River
Umatilla Reef, 99-101, 102
Umatilla, OR, 116
United Nations, 65
University of Puget Sound, 137
University of Washington (Seattle),
    14, 18, 24, 132, 133; Raitt Hall
    (Commons), 14; Board of Regents
    of, 14, 15; scientists, 43, 53-55;
    and nuclear testing in Marshall
    Islands, 76

Vallentyne, Howard, 29
Van Vliet, Joe, 116-17
Vancouver Island, BC, 100, 102
Vancouver, Capt. George, 117
Vantage, WA, 135
Victoria, BC, 99
Vietnam War, 61, 76-77
Volcanic eruptions, 125; *see also*
    Mount St. Helens

Walla Walla River, 117
Walla Walla Valley, 3
Wallula Gap, 117
Walsh, Mike, 16
Washington coast, 99, 121
Washington State University
    (Washington State College,
    Pullman), 4, 130; *The Evergreen*

(student newspaper), 4; scientists, 50, 79
Waterville Tramway, 139-40
Waterville, WA, 3, 140
Wenatchee, WA, 138, 139
Westby, Ole, 16
White Bluffs, WA, 127
White, Alice, 61
Whitman County, WA, 88
Wilkinson, Capt. Eugene P., 108
Willapa Bay, WA, 41-42
Williams, Alma, 2
Williams, Christie Simpson, 1-4
Williams, Hill Sr., 1-2, 4-6, 19, 23, 25
Williams, Mary Louise Corbett, 36, 95, 129, 136, 137; trading roles with Hill, 44-47; in Japan, 168
Williams, Milton, 2

Williams, Tom, 128-29
Williams, Ursula Trainor, 4-5, 51
Williams, Wendell, 2
Williams, William L., 1-4
Wilson Creek, WA, 1-2
World War I, 106
World War II, 27, 32, 52; submarines, 106; Hanford's role in, 121, 127; delay of Columbia Basin Irrigation Project, 123; and Japan, 167-70
Worth, Captain Frank, 99

Yakima River, 51
Yakima, WA, 44
Yang, Skinny Y. C., 144-45
Year of the Coast, 128